Pre-Owned Fashion Startup: How to Start a Business Selling Vintage, Name Brand, Used & Upcycled Fashion

Includes Advice on How to Sell on eBay, Amazon FBA, Etsy, Shopify, VarageSale & More

By

Marian Robinson

Parma Books

Cover & Book Design by Jennifer Rothschild

Contents

Intro: On Gran and Her Fashion Sense

"Don't be afraid to pile on the layers, dear. You'll catch your death out there."

Gran had always been obsessed with layers. In her mind, it was as if I was always running around barefoot and topless in the yard with a garden hose in my hand like I was perpetually five years old. Apparently, I never grew into a mature, responsible adult, perfectly aware that I need to wear the right kind of clothes if I didn't want to catch a cold. It was hardwired into her brain that I needed to be told to wear layers because I couldn't be trusted to do so myself.

But the thing about Gran's layers was that she didn't just want me to wear any layer. She wanted me to wear fashionable layers. She's hip, she's groovy, and her wardrobe is a treasure trove of the most fabulous finds in the fashion industry, in my opinion. And she'd happily lend them to me without expecting them back.

Gran was a powerhouse of a fashionista during her time. When she passed away unexpectedly, all that I had left of her were the ghosts of her clothes hanging in her closet. I found myself forever wearing those layers because she'd always told me to.

To say that I loved and adored Gran is an understatement. She was the coolest grandmother - never neglectful, never restricting. She balanced the way she related to her grandchildren with the right mix of discipline and friendship. She had always been like that. Her impeccable sense of mixing and matching is just as unparalleled with the way she dressed. So when my mother told me one of Gran's last wishes, I was floored.

"The clothes. All of it. They're yours, honey. She always wanted you to have them."

Everything was in perfect condition—not a single coat wrinkled, not a single thread out of place. Gran valued her clothes like a collector would their prized possessions. After a tear or two and a lot of reminiscing, I took the clothes—and Gran's wishes—home with me.

Gran's clothes meant a lot to me, and I kept the really important ones that have some sentimental value I just can't put a price tag on. But rather than have the clothes grow their own mold culture in the attic, I decided to give away or sell the rest. Gran would have wanted the same thing. She had always been a strong proponent of sharing fashion – and proper layers - for everyone.

I started with just a few basic pieces that I sold to family and friends, then moved on to my own clothes. I'm quite the clothing hoarder myself, and I realized that I couldn't keep all of these pieces with me. So I sold, and I sold, and I sold. Eventually, what began as a small way of letting go of Gran's stuff ended up becoming my own second-hand clothing shop online, with a steady stream of customers and loyal fans of my distinct style.

Maybe you're going through the same thing, or you simply have a ton of clutter at home that you want to clear out. Maybe you've gone full Marie Kondo and want to live a minimalist life, or maybe you just want some way to make a quick buck from home. Whatever your end goal may be, there's no doubt about it—second-hand retail is a booming industry, and for a good reason.

While starting your own business from scratch sounds pretty daunting, I can tell you that as long as you're equipped with the right knowledge and a lot of hard work (plus a little bit of luck under your belt), you can safely navigate through the second-hand retail industry and maybe even make it big afterward.

I wrote this book to help you do just that. Using the most straightforward, factual, and useful information from first-hand experience and a ton of research when I was first starting out, I've compiled this handy guide that's chockfull of the right knowledge for you to take the leap. From practical steps on how to take the right photos that will attract customers to your used clothing shop to the necessary legal stuff that will help get your business up and running, this book is your one-stop-shop to get you started on your preloved clothing industry journey.

So, suit up, and let's begin!

The Second-hand Clothing Industry Today

According to Thredup's data, the second-hand market is steadily growing and will continue to grow exponentially over the next five years. The used market will reach $51B, with the total preloved apparel market to double. Over the past three years, the resale market has expanded 21 times quicker than regular retail apparel, as more and more women (a whopping 64%) become more willing to purchase second-hand goods.

Part of this appeal is the thrill of a good bargain. The hunt drives people of all ages and incomes to buy second-hand, including luxury shoppers. In 2018 alone, approximately

56M women bought used products, which is 44M greater than the statistics from the previous year.

Another big reason for this spike is the birth of the Instagram generation. With OOTDs going viral, more and more consumers feel the need to post fabulous new Outfits of the Day for their loyal followers. There's a constant need to be seen wearing new styles that switch up every now and then.

To top it off, an impressive 74% of sustainably conscious consumers aged 18-29 want to support sustainable and more eco-friendly options when it comes to their clothing, hence, the boost in second-hand clothes. The simple act of purchasing a used item can already help reduce carbon footprint by 82%.

This emerging market is good news for thrift enthusiasts— no longer do they have to scour the country for diamonds in the rough. Mom-and-pop shops no longer have exclusivity when it comes to second-hand and vintage clothing—it's now easier than ever to find the perfect retro clothes both online and in brick-and-mortar stores. Now that consignment sites are on the rise, digital deals are selling like hotcakes more than ever.

Of course, there will always be the big brands out there that still have a huge chunk of the market. The consignment industry in the United States alone is already worth billions, with over 16 billion dollars. More than 25,000 registered consignment and resale shops have opened across the States, and the industry is only expected to grow with a steady 7% growth.

If you're thinking that it's going to be a huge mountain to scale to be able to enter such a seemingly saturated market, think again. The growing industry only means there are more and more opportunities for expansion, and new players are always welcome. Sites like Etsy and Poshmark are only two of the avenues where you can sell your used wares, and you'll find that there are surprisingly a lot of people who will find value in what you sell. You'll be pleasantly surprised to discover just how much you can price something as people are willing to take them off your hands for a good deal.

If those numbers aren't enough to convince you to join the bandwagon and get on board, I don't know what will!

First Things First

Like with any worthwhile endeavor, it's important to know how you'll be going about your business plan. Having a solid map of where you want to go and how you plan on getting there is not only good common sense—it also makes sure that you don't end up with a dead-end in the middle of nowhere after a lot of wasted time and effort.

Have a Plan

Some things you have to accept include the fact that your start-up costs will be inevitable. The good news is that with used clothing, you can cut those costs a significant amount compared to other start-ups because your starting inventory will likely be donated (or in my case, inherited). You will probably have a higher profit margin, too—most of your inventory will either be consigned or acquired for a lower price.

Another plus, when it comes to used clothing shops, is that you will still likely thrive even when economic growth is slow. No matter how fancy the clothes might be, they will always be priced considerably lower than brand new items, and in a less performing economy, people will want to tighten their belts a little bit and opt for used rather than new.

That said, here are the things you need to consider when you're drafting your business plan.

Know your customer

This is one of the most important things to determine in any business and not just in the retail industry. Who is your target market? Whom do you want to sell to? Who is your core customer? There will be a wide range of demographics to choose from, and with the used clothing industry, the sky's the limit, really. But it's important to have laser focus, especially when you're still starting out. You don't want to get overwhelmed by all of the options you have out there—after all, you can't target everybody.

This is actually one of the biggest rookie mistakes business noobs fall into. When faced with the question of who their target market is, the answer is often a disappointing, "Everybody." I mean, sure, it's okay to dream big—after all, everybody wears clothes, right? Not only does this kind of mindset set you up for failure, but it also makes you lose focus when it comes to the big business decisions you will eventually have to make.

For instance, when setting up your logo, your branding, and your overall image, having an "everybody" target market will leave you with a disjointed approach to your brand. If you go for a clean and minimalist approach with small fonts and not much else, the texts may be difficult to read and might be a turn-off for the older bracket. If you go with vibrant colors and larger-than-life icons with bold combinations of clothes, this may not attract the more conservative consumers who just want traditional top-and-bottom pairs.

As for the clothes themselves, you may target fashionistas who want to get on board with the latest fashion trends but don't want to break the bank when it comes to luxury brands. You may also target old-school hearts that have a particular nostalgia for times gone by. These consumers will likely be more into vintage clothing styles, which will dictate how you position yourself in the market as well as how you create your brand image. This will also determine how you will go about your advertising and marketing plan, which we'll discuss in this book as well.

When trying to find out who your target market is, make sure you determine their basic demographics like their age group as well as their lifestyles. I'll get into more detail about this in the next few sections.

Location, location, location

If you're planning on setting up shop the brick-and-mortar way, location is one of the most important things you need to consider. You not only have to scour the whole metro to find the right place to sell your wares (this will also tie into whom your target market will be), but you will also need to balance rental rates and foot traffic.

Once you do find the perfect place for you, keep in mind that you don't have to be bound by one physical location alone. Your storefront isn't the only place you can sell and make money—you can also go online or participate in bazaars and flea markets. Swap meets are also a good place to get good deals, so be on the lookout for these events in your area.

If you haven't decided on a good location, or you don't have enough funds to rent just yet, you can first get a sense of the local market with these regular events. Bazaars are a good way to test the waters and to see how the locals will react to your wares. This will also help you build a steady following even before you set up shop.

Marketing plan

They say that big Hollywood blockbusters allot 50% of their budget to marketing, and for a good reason. Again, this will tie into your target market, as to how you advertise will also be based on your target consumer's demographics, lifestyles, and preferences. What makes your brand unique? How do you want yourself to be seen? How do you want to position yourself in the market? When people think about your company, how do you want them to perceive your products?

High-quality market research can be pretty expensive, but they will help you get on the right track before you even begin. When you think about your marketing plan, think about your company's Strengths, Weaknesses, Opportunities, and Threats (this is also known as a SWOT analysis). This will help you determine a lot of key factors before you open your doors. It's good to know about your competitors as well and see how they're doing. You can learn from the best and try to adapt their styles with yours.

There are plenty of online resources you can look into if you want some professional help drafting your marketing plan if you have the funds to spare.

Budgeting and costs

Speaking of funds, you have to take into consideration all of your finances realistically. Unless you've got tons and tons of money lying around, you have to be judicious when it comes to where and how you spend your money, especially as a start-up.

For instance, with an online store, you will have to factor in your monthly rent and utility expenses into your budget. You will need to buy starting equipment for your clothing store (we will talk more about this later), as well as an employee or two to help man the booth or the register for you. With your employees, you need to know the requirements of law when it comes to insurance and payroll taxes. This is all on top of the capital you need to invest in acquiring your main inventory (the clothes!) in the first place.

As a rough estimate, you can expect to shell out about $2,000 - $10,000 in start-up costs, depending on how you handle your preferences. You need to have a significant amount of cash ready and on-hand. If you need to borrow money to help you get started, you may be able to get financing help from well-meaning family and friends, partners, or even banks.

Don't be afraid to spend a little to get started, but don't go overboard with your expenses, either. This is why it helps to have a projected business plan to see how your revenues will fare further down the road so that you can safely shell out the right amount of cash to start your business.

Determine Your Customer Base

Because one of the most important things you will need to cement in stone is your target market, I can help you with some tactics on determining your customer base. There's a high level of competition in the market because of its profitability, but that also means there's a wide range of niches you can focus on when setting up shop.

Some of the most well-known brands in the market include:

Poshmark	ThredUp	Trunk Show Consignment	Second Time Around
Cadillac's Castle	Michael's Consignment	The Dressing Room	Buffalo Exchange
Beacon's Closet	The RealReal	Crossroads Trading Co	ThreadFlip
Encore	Twice	A&E Clothing	

Thankfully, there's enough room for everyone to have their own share of the pie. Just like there is no typical brand new clothes shopper, there's no typical second-hand clothes customer, either. Regardless of financial status or economic background, a consumer will likely buy your used clothes if you hit the mark just right.

However, if finding exactly what makes a customer tick is a walk in the park, then there would be no failed businesses at all, would there? Finding the sweet spot and being able to provide the perfect solution to your customer's very specific needs entails a lot of hard work.

Thankfully, there are many online resources where you can conduct surveys without ever having to leave your home. Simply search your favorite search engine on survey providers and you will be presented with a bunch of options with different packages. Some will restrict the number of respondents, while some will have features like logic branches to provide you with the most accurate answers from participants the world over.

In my opinion, the best feasibility studies and market research come from doing actual, manual footwork. You can go around asking people and doing surveys from real people in the streets or in your own social circle. Economic analysis—and an accurate one at that—is never an easy thing to do, and you have to do due diligence to get it right. Think about place, product, promotion, and pricing (the four Ps) when you're determining your target market.

Now, at this point, it's well worth mentioning the option of buying a franchise. As opposed to starting from scratch, a franchise will already have a target market set up for you. Still, you will probably be able to expand with much more freedom if you start from scratch. It will all really depend on your business vision and your end-goals. The freedom that your own brand provides is invaluable when it comes to making business decisions that you feel is right for you as opposed to being bound by the shackles of an already existing franchise.

How to Conduct Market Research

There's no doubt that building your clothing brand by using your own personal preferences has its perks, but the hard truth is that you can't simply thrive without studying what the consumer wants. You need to take into consideration the local market factors as well as typical customer behavior.

How can you sell products that speak to your customers directly? How do you reflect the fashion choices of the market? You can do first-hand data collection via focus groups, one-on-one interviews, group surveys, and even ads from Facebook Audience Insights. A huge benefit of speaking to your customers directly is the fact that you can really understand them and add follow-up questions if you need to.

If you feel like this is too tedious or difficult for you, you can spare some funds and hire third-party market research agencies to do the work for you. You can bank on their years of experience in the field using the most tried-and-tested methodologies and best practices. They can be the most efficient way to getting the most comprehensive data on the industry, but they tend to be more costly.

You can also do secondary research from case studies, reports, and public documentation. You can check publications like Nielsen, statistics, and research from other agencies and trade associations. Your local chamber of commerce will also likely have some info you don't have to pay for. If you're on a tight budget, your local library or the World Wide Web is a good place to start. For instance, ThomasNet is an online resource that helps to connect sellers and buyers in various industries.

You can access a wealth of information about consumer markets by joining trade associations. You can also check the Statistical Abstract of the United States, as well as the Encyclopedia of Associations (Gale Cengage Learning).

It's important to get a good grasp of the current and future trends as well as buying patterns in the market. You can also turn to the U.S. Census Bureau for free business data on localized units and statistics for various metropolitan areas. The Census Product Update also provides information on upcoming items from the U.S. Census Bureau.

Local business schools, colleges, and universities can provide research on sales, marketing, strategic planning, and other kinds of financial information. Businesses like D&B can specifically help start-ups with directories for consultants, regional businesses, and service companies.

As for the survey itself, here are some sample questions you can ask to begin:

- What is your age?

- What is your gender?

- When you're buying clothes, where do you usually shop?

- How much are you willing to pay for a typical top?

- What is more important to you when buying clothes: the design or the brand?

- When do you usually shop for clothes? (Indicate seasons)

- What are your style influences? Check all that apply. (Include friends, family, trends, media)

- What are your criteria when buying clothes? Rank from highest to lowest. (Include style, color, price, brand, ads)

- What is the main reason you buy clothes?

- What is your favorite color?

- How much do you spend on clothing items every year?

- What is your profession?

- How much is your income range?

You can also do a more comprehensive type of survey, with respondents agreeing in varying levels about each statement. Answers would be Disagree, Somewhat Disagree, Neutral, Somewhat Agree, Agree. Examples of statements would be:

- I value affordability above all else.

- I check the brand first before I buy anything.

- My friends think I am a trendsetter and have good fashion sense.

- Regardless of what's currently trending, I buy the clothes and designs that appeal to me specifically.

- I'm not as concerned about what other people think of what I'm wearing.

- I value comfort above all else.

- I am more of a modest dresser.

- I am very confident in my own fashion style.

- I love to buy clothes even if I don't have an immediate need for them.

- I only buy clothes if I need them for a special occasion.

- I only buy clothes if my old ones are already worn out.

- I only buy clothes if my favorite public personality or influencer endorses them.

- I'm not afraid to set my own style.

- I'm not a fan of mainstream styles and I prefer to create my own.

- I feel really good when I buy new clothes.

- I only buy clothes that flatter my figure specifically.

- I am an impulse buyer.

- I only buy clothes when they go on sale.

- I want to wear something new every day.

- I don't mind repeating my clothes every few days.

- I don't want to wear mass-produced clothes and I only want unique pieces.

- I feel bad when someone else is wearing the same thing I am.

- I prefer online over physical stores.

- I prefer physical stores over online shops.

- I don't feel safe when paying for purchases online.

- I want to make sure the clothes fit first before I buy them.

- I don't mind buying online as long as there is a good return policy.

As you can see, there are tons of questions you can ask your potential customer to be able to learn their behaviors and cater to their needs specifically. You can also create a survey for after-sales services to know how you can improve as a brand. Questions may include:

- How likely are you to recommend this clothing brand?

- Did you encounter any problems while checking out or purchasing?

- How well does this item specifically meet your needs?

- What do you want to add for improvement?

- What did you like best about this item?

- What did you like least about this item?

- What made you choose this brand over another clothing competitor?

- How would you rate your shopping experience?

Make sure you don't get side-tracked by the many answers you'll get—stick to your business plan and only compile the relevant answers for your brand.

All About the Clothes

Here comes the most important part—the clothes themselves! Selling used clothes is all about the used clothes. You should know where to source them, what your options are, and the best practices you should try to follow when selling original and high-quality goods.

Building Your Inventory: Where to Source

Since you'll be selling used clothes, you might think that it's a given as to where you need to source your clothes. After all, you're selling pre-loved items, and you've either inherited them or they're yours to begin with. But if you're going to be expanding your business, you can't stick to limited inventory such as your personal effects and those of your loved ones.

A good, reliable supplier is always an important backbone of any retail business. The advantage of selling used clothes is that you don't have to rely on a single source—you can build your inventory from a wide range of sources out there if you just know where to look!

Garage sales are a good source of second-hand clothing. Lots of families or communities hold regular garage sales, and these are magical treasure troves of places where you can score really good deals. Make sure that you inspect the quality of each item, as garage sales may not always have the best presentation when it comes to merchandise display. You need to have a keen eye on how to spot a good bargain. Make sure that you check the price tag and try to haggle if you can. The price tags are normally negotiable—do your best to lower the price but don't be unreasonable. Nobody likes a Scrooge!

When you've scoured all of the garage sales in your neighborhood, you can venture a little bit outside of your own immediate vicinity and check flea markets. These events normally have a lot of booths selling exactly that—second-hand clothes. Eventually, this will also be one of your sales channels for when you want to expand or join bazaars. Flea markets are a great way to reach out to your existing customers and gain new ones—but we'll get more into that in the later chapters of this book.

If you've got the time and the energy for it, you can also go from house to house to source used clothes. You need to have some form of manpower or an assistant to help you do this, as you can't possibly make the rounds to and from each household on your own. Most of the time, people are more than willing to donate if you tell them you'll take their clutter off their hands. Be honest and transparent—you don't want to come off as a scam or duplicitous. Be creative, be polite, and make sure you know how to handle them saying "no."

If you've got the funds for it, you can also place an ad in the local newspaper. You can offer free pickups to make the experience as hassle-free as possible for the donor. You can also place these ads online—just remember that the merch you might receive won't always be in the best condition. They say that one man's trash is another man's treasure, but sometimes, people can give away things that really have no value whatsoever.

You can also be on the lookout for clothing shops that are already deciding to liquidate their businesses. They will normally have closing out sales at ridiculously low prices just to get rid of their existing inventory. Be ready to hunt for the best deals that will yield the most profit for you.

When sourcing your inventory, it also helps if you're a sociable type of person. You can befriend your local recyclers, or your neighborhood tailors and dressmakers. You just might find the lifeblood of your business from raiding not just your family and friends' closets but those of clothing clinics as well.

Online auction sites can also be a good option. Places like Craigslist and eBay can sometimes have high-quality designer labels on sale, with price reductions of as much as 70%. The important thing you should remember is that you should know the original price—or at least be aware of its current market value on an average—before you buy and resell. Do your homework—well-known brands will have their own websites, so even if you can't head to their physical stores, you can already easily check their prices online from the comfort of your own home.

What Is Consignment, Anyway?

What is consignment and how does it work? This refers to the age-old practice of selling goods whereby the consignor retains ownership of items while they are on display. It's an arrangement between the owner and the seller. The product is placed in a store's care until it is eventually bought by a customer. The shop or the consignee will pay the owner a pre-agreed price once the item is bought by a buyer.

Based on the proceeds of the sale, the owner of the item and the shop each get a certain percentage as they split the earnings from the sale. Small businesses and start-ups can take advantage of this kind of arrangement especially since beginners normally don't have huge spaces to fill up with inventory just yet. If you are the consignee, you can also take full advantage of this arrangement as you can have your items on display in bigger stores simply by agreeing on a consignment percentage to strengthen your stock.

The bigger store will essentially sell your items on your behalf. You not only get shelf space, but you also get to ride on the popularity and positioning or location of the bigger store that sells your item. This raises brand awareness, which is invaluable especially when you're just starting out. It can help you sell your products without having an actual physical storefront just yet. You basically save up on rent and payroll for employees.

The downside of this, of course, is the fact that you have to share part of your earnings with the shop that displays your product. You don't get the full sale, but this percentage is actually what you essentially "pay" the shop for selling your products for you.

If staying liquid is important to you, consignment doesn't provide you with that luxury. You don't get the money until the item gets sold. You need to plan your cash flow carefully to allot for these. Security may also be an issue, as you are entrusting the safety of your goods to the store. If they get damaged or stolen, you don't really have that much control over it. Make sure that you review all of these provisions when you enter into a consignment agreement.

More than the price percentages, you should take into consideration security, display space, shelf location, notifications if an item becomes out of stock, terms of payment, and whether or not the store will help in promoting your products. For instance, their in-store staff must be well-trained enough to know how to market or explain your product or item to an inquiring customer that walks in.

What Types of Clothing to Sell

There are literally limitless kinds of clothing items you can sell. While you may want to cover all of your bases and sell everything under the sun, having a focus will give you heaps and heaps of help especially when you're just starting out. You can always expand to more types of clothes as your business grows, but as a start-up, it's important to know where to focus first.

Vintage

What is considered vintage clothing? This can be anything that's 20-100 years old, and is usually indicative of its era. It should showcase the specific trends and styles during that particular period of time. Used vintage clothes can include any number of styles, and what's considered "vintage" is always changing, always evolving. When vintage clothing surpasses the 100-year mark, it becomes an antique.

Vintage shouldn't be confused with classic clothing, which is something that's stylish regardless of the passing of time. It doesn't showcase a particular era's style—it transcends eras, in fact. Classics include trench coats, the LBD (little black dress), pumps, blazers, and white button-down shirts.

For vintage, the 1920s saw flapper dresses, heeled Mary Janes, and long beads—these would be vintage clothing today. For the 30s, it was puffed and fluttery sleeves, oxfords, bolero jackets, fedoras, peep-toe footwear, and sling backs. During the 40s, reptile handbags, reptile shoes, brooches, tweed and wool plaid skirts, and platform shoes were all the rage.

In the 50s, there were twin sweater sets, shirtwaist dresses, petticoats, fur trim, and the Wayfarer sunglasses. Pillbox hats and bell bottom jeans were a huge thing in the 60s, while flare jeans, block heels, thigh-high boots, and boho-chic styles dominated the 70s. As for the 80s, who can forget gold chains and shoulder pads, then baggy flannel shirts and chokers in the 90s?

If you want to sell vintage clothing, you should make sure you check actual vintage shops for curated collections. Make sure that the ones you source should still be easily paired with contemporary pieces, just so you can broaden your horizons.

It's also important to note that the different sizes then may no longer be applicable to the sizes today. Women's dress sizes have significantly evolved as the years have gone by. Always compare vintage pieces with new pieces to check for any changes. For instance, a size 6 today would be an estimated size 12 in the 60s, more or less.

Upcycled

If you haven't heard of upcycled clothing before, that's okay—it's a growing trend that will likely keep growing as the years go by. It basically means making use of pieces that already exist, effectively going a more sustainable route when it comes to what you're wearing. It turns "unwanted" items back into "wanted" again for a limited use of resources.

Clothes can have an afterlife if you don't immediately discard them as trash. In 2012 alone, an estimated 14.3 million tons of textiles were discarded to the landfill as reported by the Environmental Protection Agency—an alarming number for something seemingly harmless as discarding old clothes.

With upcycling, you can still make use of something that's torn, damaged, or stained and refashion it into something fabulous. Even while a piece of clothing is being manufactured, it can already be upcycled in a sense—the leftover fabric from cutting out patterns can be repurposed. From the post-consumer waste end, a shirt that no longer fits can be fashioned into something else—all you need is a little bit of imagination and creativity. Even upholstery scraps or vintage textiles can still have new life, as well as worn-out clothes and tattered pieces.

For instance, the grunge look is all the rage right now with semi-tattered items that have been repurposed. Men's work shirts can be fashioned into girls' dresses, while denim remnants can still make for chic handbags. Upcycling not only helps Mother Earth, but it also appeals to a sense of nostalgia and sentimentality for many customers. Items become more memorable as creatives breathe new life into them.

If you're planning on selling upcycled clothes, you can try your hand at making them yourself, or selling them for the creatives who make them. You can position yourself as an eco warrior as you sell these environmentally conscious clothes to make the world a better—and more fashionable—place.

Ideas for upcycling clothes:

- Make a man's shirt into a little girl's dress.
- Upcycle an old sweater into a scarf.
- Turn an old denim skirt into a vest.
- Add lace to the edge of tattered shirts to bring them back to life.
- Go crazy with a bleach pen to add designs to dark fabrics.

Condition and Counterfeits

Whatever you decide to sell, keep in mind that you are NOT a scammer. You should always value integrity and your customers' trust in you, especially as you build toward brand loyalty. Make sure that you provide quality products. Just because they're used doesn't mean they have to be worn-out!

Treat all of those garments the way they should be treated. Keep in mind that used clothing shouldn't have to LOOK used. Make sure that they are clean, wrinkle-free, and appealing—you will attract more customers this way. Users will also be more likely to leave good reviews or recommend you via word of mouth to their family and friends. They might just become a repeat customer, which is hitting the jackpot as far as customer loyalty is concerned.

Take the time to remove stains or smells. Wash them, steam them, and iron them. Do so before you take photos of the garments or before you display them if you have a physical store. You want to make sure that you present them like they are brand new, but you should never say that they are! They're still second-hand goods, but they should LOOK totally new.

If the fabrics are more delicate, make sure you do the proper research on how to wash or handle them with the utmost care. This is especially true if you're going to sell vintage items—that beautiful dress from the 40s probably won't do so well in the washing machine. Make sure that all of the buttons are complete and that seams are intact. Then, store them with care in bins or racks.

When it comes to brand integrity, you should know counterfeit goods, replicas, and knockoffs like the back of your hand. There are different provisions in place and a myriad of penalties for anyone who breaks the law against intellectual property rights. While the fast-paced world of the Internet can make fake products easily accessible, that doesn't mean you should join the bandwagon and be part of the trend.

Legal repercussions are vast. It can be difficult to figure out originals from fakes, but when you're sourcing your inventory, you should be doubly careful. For instance, counterfeit goods infringe upon trademarks directly. They are meant to be deceptive, with the end goal of making a customer think that it is an original. Replicas, on the other hand, can be similar to an original but are not exact copies. They normally don't have the original logo, or can have subtle differences in design.

Most big e-commerce websites have safeguards against illegal items. Even replicas and knock-offs are prohibited on platforms like Amazon and eBay. Not abiding by the rules of e-commerce platforms may lead to withheld funds, suspension of your account, or the disposal of your products.

It's important to abide by the rules and regulations of your chosen platforms if you don't want to get banned. Normally, you should only have one registered seller account, and you should provide honest information that's accurate and true at all times. Steer clear of prohibited products (you can find guidelines on these depending on your chosen e-commerce platform). This includes being absolutely clear about the condition of your items. Since you're selling used clothes, be sure to indicate that they are used. You should never try to pass them off as brand new.

Your identification and credentials will also be verified in most cases, just to ensure that you are a legitimate seller. This will show your customers that you are a reliable and trustworthy seller. Don't worry—this is for your own benefit.

Let's Get Down to Business

Yes, starting your own clothing store is fun and exciting, but the reality is that it's not all just fun and games. You should also be savvy enough to handle the serious business side of things, which often isn't as glamorous. If you're already a biz whiz, then that's great—but chances are you're just a regular layman who has no idea where to begin. Don't fret—I've got you.

Going Online

There's a whole bunch of things to consider, but first things first—where exactly do you want to sell your second-hand clothes? You've got two main options: you can either go the online route, or go for the traditional brick-and-mortar shop. You can always do both—in fact, a majority of businesses out there have both an offline and an online channel to help maximize sales. But for the sake of simplicity right now, let's talk about each option first in great detail.

Going online means you've got a limitless range of sales channels to choose from. New marketplaces are popping up here and there, and it can be overwhelming to pick the right one. Let's break it down bit by bit, shall we?

ThredUP

Yes, I know you're starting your own used clothing business, but for the sake of discussion, let's talk about ThredUP. This growing site does the selling for you—you send them your used clothes and their second-hand experts will weigh in on how much the clothes are worth. You have the option of receiving payment online or donating your sales to charity. It's not exactly a way for you to really start your own used clothing biz, but it's a quick way to sell old clothes. You can maybe try to use this as a testing ground to see how much certain items can be worth, and if there is any value to them.

One of the good things to note about ThredUP is that if you want to get your unsold items back, you can request a return and they'll send them back to you for a minimal fee.

Poshmark

This social platform is basically an easily downloadable app where you can sell your clothes across a network. You get shipping assistance and priority boxes from USPS for a 20% fee. Since you'll be relying on networks to get the word out, it' important to build a following as well as share posts from other people to make sure that there's enough interest buzzing around. Prices are negotiable too, so knowing how to haggle is a huge plus.

Aside from making sure that you take amazing photos of your clothes (use natural light as much as possible), you need to write really good descriptions that are accurate and thorough. Make sure that you clearly indicate the fabric content, the exact condition, and the measurements. Be ready to input keywords about what makes your clothing item so great. It will also help if you've got nifty tricks and trips on how to keep those garments in good condition depending on the fabric, so that your customer will happily wear their satisfying purchase for years to come.

eBay

eBay allows you to sell items for a higher price, as you control everything from scratch. This is also its own con though, as you need to be prepared to do all the work. This is a great option for sellers who have rare treasures. You can receive higher profits as the site's service fees are relatively more affordable than other channels. Still, eBay is a little old-school, and some of the functionalities are a little bit clunky.

With eBay, you have the option of selling your items at a fixed price, or starting an auction. You can set a beginning price and customers can start bidding during a limited period of time. In my opinion, going for a fixed price is more effective, at least in my experience. Just make sure that all of your listings are complete, accurate, and descriptive.

Make sure you get the keywords in there, and polish everything to make it look professional. The way your listings work will greatly affect buying decisions, and if your item looks professional, it'll give users a sense of security and make them believe that you're not a scam. There's always a level of anonymity when doing transactions online, but if you make sure that your listing is at the top of its game, you can reduce that uneasy feeling for customers and make them feel comfortable buying your stuff.

Depop

If you've got a lot of vintage clothes and quirky accessories, Depop will probably be your best bet. A mix between Instagram and eBay, Depop caters to the younger market for teens and early 20-somethings. Having the best photos and descriptions is an absolute must. Another key to succeeding in this platform is to make sure you have the right hashtags that are relevant to your brand or your clothes. This is probably what comes closest to opening your own store, only there's a 10% fee on your sales.

Facebook Marketplace

If you've been around the social media scene for a while now, there's a huge chance that you already have a Facebook account. Marketplace is just an extension where you can sell used clothes (and anything under the sun!) to customers around your area. It's a great way to reach out to those who have close proximity to your location. A huge plus is how convenient it is to sell something—you literally just have to click the button that says, "Sell Something".

Another big advantage that Facebook Marketplace has over other sales channels online is that selling stuff is absolutely free. It's like an online classifieds section where you can post any listing you might have. Potential buyers can reach out to you upon seeing your listing, and you can arrange for particular transactions and terms of payment afterward. When an item is sold, you can mark them as such in your listing.

It doesn't provide that much safety when it comes to the actual transactions, as these are done privately. Arrangements are purely between you and the customer, and are done outside of Facebook. Both the seller and the customer can't really be a hundred percent protected from bogus deals. You have to do due diligence to make sure you don't get scammed and vice versa. There's no seller protection or buyer protection in place, and no rating system for both parties, either.

Tradesy

Convenience is the name of the game with Tradesy. Here, you can sell not only used clothes but also accessories, handbags, and anything that goes along with your preloved goods. Simply list your goods on the website. Then, when you make a sale, you will receive a prepaid package that you can send to your customer. You also have the option of printing your own shipping label from wherever you're based.

It's a convenient way to sell anything you have in your closet, but the downside is that the fees can be a little steep, especially for someone who's just starting out. The website takes a $7.50 commission per item for products priced under $50. Anything more than that amount will be charged a 19.8% commission. You have to be prepared to factor this into your selling price, or at least know how you can recover from the fees and still make a reasonable profit.

Vinted

What sets Vinted apart from other online marketplaces is probably its bundling feature. It's easy to de-clutter or sell even high-fashion brands with the free listings—all you have to do is pay for postage, which will depend on the package size of your items. Bundling lets customers buy things in bulk along with varying price adjustments. You can also offer a bunch of discounts or promotions to make sure that you stand out from the other used clothing sellers in the market.

Instagram

Everyone is doing it, and for good reason—Instagram has definitely grown over the years from a social media platform to an online marketplace as well. Today, IG is no longer just for posting photos of your pets, your meals, or your OOTDs. It can also be used as a highly effective tool to sell anything under the sun, and used clothing is no exception.

If you've got that indomitable entrepreneurial spirit and you know how to keep a steady and solid following, then you just might thrive in your Instagram account. As long as you have the passion and the drive, plus a hint of creativity, you can excel at selling used clothing in this fast-paced social media platform.

Instagram accounts are free, and they don't charge any commission or percentage on what you're selling. You have complete control over your content, from photos to descriptions to wow-worthy hashtags. The challenge here is that almost everyone else is selling their stuff on Instagram, so you have to find a way to stand out from the crowd.

It's not easy to drive customers to your page, but when is attracting customers to any business ever easy? The very first thing you need to do is know how to take the most jaw-dropping photos and stunning flat lays. You can use hashtags like #instacloset, #shopmycloset, #clothesforsale, or #instasale among others to get customers to check out your wares.

Since Instagram doesn't have its own payment gateway like other e-commerce websites, it's a good idea to have

PayPal set up to make sure you can handle online transactions with your customers. Some deals will also be made outside of Instagram and will be private between you and your buyer, so always practice caution when dealing with payments privately.

There are also best practices when you're setting up shop on Instagram. Always be honest, provide complete information, and make sure your photos are accurate. You technically have over one billion potential customers on Instagram, and they're all very much engaged. You have to make your posts targeted even without the need to buy Instagram paid ads.

Still, if you have the funds to spare for paid ads, you can make use of the tools in Instagram for Business. Aside from making sure that your visual content is amazing, it's also important to get creative—use photos, videos, and clips or GIFs to portray your message. You can also showcase what you're selling via Instagram Stories. These short clips feature a slideshow format and can only be visible for 24 hours. If you want to keep them around after a day, you can add them to your page's Highlights to make sure they stick around.

For IG stories, you can post behind-the-scenes stuff that may be interesting for your customers. Maybe you can post something new you've sourced, or show yourself hunting for good deals at a bazaar. You can talk about the history of the clothes you already have on hand—customers love a personal story or an interesting anecdote. You can also tag other partner accounts (or users and influencers!) in your stories. Stories have features like stickers, face filters, hashtags, polls, and other Call-To-Action buttons. It's a fun and useful way of engaging with your followers even more.

Of course, the most important thing is to have a winning profile that people will actually want to click. Make sure that the clickable link in your bio is working and relevant (it could be your own website if you have one). This can also be a link to a promotion, a limited-time event, a subscription to a newsletter, and so on.

Instagram Business profiles also provide extra analytics data for your customers. You can measure results with engagements and clicks. These can be super valuable when it comes to studying your market. You can refine your market or expand your reach, or study how your existing customers behave. This will help you fine-tune any future posts to make sure you get the best engagement possible.

Another technique you can use on Instagram is to collaborate with other users and sellers. You can even align with non-profit organizations for regular events. You can also do a shout-out for increased exposure—just make sure that you partner with brands and influencers that have similar ideals and an aligned vision with yours. Remember:

relevant followers who actually convert to sales are more important than just having thousands of followers who lurk around and do nothing.

Once you get a good grasp of your followers on IG, you can reward their loyalty and interest with exclusive perks and build toward anticipation for your clothes. Give them exclusive access, sneak peeks, and teaser posts of the latest releases or newest store openings. This will make your followers feel special because they have the inside scoop.

Instagram is a mammoth of a beast to handle, but you will eventually get the hang of it. It's not a be-all-end-all, either—you can have an Instagram account and still have other selling platforms that you can maximize. Don't go around signing up for every online platform you can get your hands on, either—just focus on a key few that will bring you the most success.

Craigslist

Just because something is old-fashioned doesn't mean it's out of date. Craigslist is still one of the most effective places online where you can sell practically anything. It's not exactly flashy or fancy, but it does the job, and does it well. This reliable tool connects you with customers directly and opens your store up to more profits since there are no fees.

Mercari

You can take advantage of the prepaid labels in Mercari to keep your shipping costs on the lower side. The buyer has the option of shouldering the shipping fees, with three days to return an item. Fees are at 10%, and there's a rating system in place for buyers as well as sellers. This is a nifty little feature to make sure you avoid bogus buyers.

LePrix

Feeling fancy? LePrix has an intense authentication process to make sure that only the most luxurious items in the best condition get through. You can request for a consignment kit, but make sure that your items are in excellent condition. Other regular hand-me-downs might not make the cut, so it's best to sell them somewhere else.

The Real Real

You can also consign high-end fashion items here, from brands like Chanel, Gucci, Prada, etc. you can earn anywhere from 55% to 70% of the price of the item. You can consign your items and the site will do the photography, pricing, and selling for you.

Grailed

Here's an interesting example of a niche market—Grailed is geared toward men who want to de-clutter their closet. You can sell clothes and accessories as well; with four categories you can break down your wares into. Grails is meant for more high-end designers, while Core is for the more mainstream brands. This includes Zara, Levi's, H&M, Uniqlo, and so on. Hype is for new releases that are "hyped", while Sartorial is for classic menswear that are more on the high-end side.

The website charges 6% commission for every item that you sell. Add that to applicable PayPal fees depending on your location or currency. You should know how to factor in these costs into your final sale price.

VarageSale

Ever heard of a yard sale done online? VarageSale helps you sell all kinds of stuff with a specifically targeted location in your area. This is a good option if you don't want to have to ship to other countries or other states. You can simply look for your local community and get verified to start.

Transactions are also done via meet-ups, but there's an added layer of security compared to Craigslist. VarageSale actually does the job of checking the identity of sellers and buyers, so you can rest easy that you won't end up dealing with random bogus people. The service is completely free of charge.

Etsy

Etsy has steadily been making a name for itself in the e-commerce industry as a place where you can score really good deals on unique and handcrafted items. If you have a lot of vintage clothing and other one-of-a-kind pieces, Etsy is your best bet. It's a crafty place for crafty people, so don't expect to sell your mainstream used clothes here. Take note of the $0.20 listing fee, plus payment processing fees from your payment gateway.

To be a successful seller on Etsy, you have to be active when it comes to engaging with the community. Try to participate in the forums, and provide feedback to other favorite sellers. Try to attend meet-ups and events in your local area. The community often organizes pop-up shops as well, so it's a great way to expand both your customers and your own network on the business end.

Aside from posting great photos in different angles under natural light, you should be aware of the right SEO keywords to use to make your products easily searchable. It's always a good idea to include relevant and descriptive keywords for your listings, but don't flood them, either! Keyword stuffing is always frowned upon, both by algorithm bots and actual human users. Having constantly updated content will also help your case in search engine rankings.

If you've got something unique that you want to share with your customers, write a couple of blog posts to talk about them. If you're more of an eco-warrior, for instance, talk about how sustainable your used clothes are. If you're a proponent of vintage items, post about the history of your goods. Always reach out to your customers by providing them with value, and not just some random sales-y stuff.

Etsy is also a great way to build brand awareness. Use your logo and branding in everything, from good packaging to calling cards you can slip into every item box or pouch. You can create a mailing list (Mailchimp is a good place to start) and interact with your customers there. Send out email campaigns to keep in touch with your customers, or inform them of new products and events you might be holding in their area.

When it comes to packaging, providing something creative and high-quality is a great way to have repeat customers. It keeps things professional and will definitely up the ante when it comes to customer satisfaction. Since you're selling used clothes, the packaging is the perfect opportunity to express your own unique stamp or your own personality.

Of course, when you finally make a sale, having great customer service is also a huge plus. Give them the option to contact you with feedback, and respond to them during a reasonable period of time. You can also try to follow-up with them to check in on them and how they're enjoying your product. You can even ask for suggestions and other comments—any good entrepreneur knows that there's always room for improvement. If they're happy and satisfied with their purchase and with you, they're more likely to recommend you to others via word-of-mouth.

Shopify

Shopify is one of the biggest e-commerce sites out there, and they provide you with easy steps on how to create your own online store. There are tons and tons of beautiful themes you can use to design your own shop easily, with simple set-up instructions and a fully functional app for sellers to make your store mobile-adaptive.

It can be pretty overwhelming at first, as Shopify provides you with hundreds of tools you can use to create your own e-commerce website. There are plenty of official guides from Shopify itself, and you should know that you'll likely be spending a huge chunk of your time going through the tutorials yourself. They're easy to navigate and understand, but you have to really dedicate some time and commit yourself to the task.

You can learn about Google integration, keyword analytics, mobile adaptive features, how to reduce abandoned carts, how to drive sales and customers to your website, how to use blog posts to increase engagement, how to add stunning free photos for commercial use, how to optimize your Shopify logo, how to upsell using recommended items to existing customers, how to reach out to lookalike audiences, and so much more! Shopify tutorials can really take up a whole new book in itself, so here's the link to the Shopify Academy to get you started.

Benefits of an Online Shop

If you do decide to go online, you'll find that there are tons of advantages you can enjoy over physical clothing stores. For one thing, start-up costs are normally cheaper than having to build an actual brick-and-mortar store; for another, you won't have to worry about finding the perfect location to sell your wares.

Online second-hand clothing stores don't require you to have a local business license, and you won't need to purchase liability insurance and other types of coverage, either. You will likely store your clothes at home if you're just starting out, so you won't need to have a physical storage space for them. Rent and staffing also won't be a problem—and these can be the biggest costs of opening a physical store.

You also won't have to worry about working hours. Your store hours will be more flexible—technically, you'll always be open, and all you have to do is update your listings whenever you have new items to sell. If you have an automated system for e-commerce, you don't even have to monitor everything every single hour of the day—you don't have to man the booth, per se.

Of course, with an online store, you need to be mindful of hosting and domain costs, as well as transaction fees for your chosen e-commerce platform. You also have to factor in your shipping costs. As for your packaging, you not only have to make sure that everything looks nice, but you also have to ensure that your packaging will hold up against any kind of mishandling during shipping.

You have to be diligent when it comes to keyword research. The right keywords and SEO knowledge will help drive customers to your online store, as you technically don't have a store frontage to let people know that you're around. For instance, the Google Keyword Planner can help you check how your business is doing keyword-wise. You should incorporate these keywords in your product names, product descriptions, and throughout your whole website.

To get started, you can create a Google AdWords Keyword Planner account and choose the "Search for new keywords" option. You can input different keywords here and check the search volume results for each. You will also see which ones provide a more targeted approach regarding relevant groups. It's a useful way of discovering new keywords as well as finding out which ones have the highest search volume. You can also check which keywords have the lowest competition.

When you've picked the keywords that you want to use, you can litter your whole website with them. Use a couple of keywords here and there and make it sound organic and not forced. You can use them in your site copy, your meta titles, your meta descriptions, your product pages, and in your social media posts.

With an online store, you can test the waters first if you're unsure about your whole business launch. You can try to gain momentum online and build a steady group of followers and loyal customers, before moving on to bigger investments like your own physical store. Because an online shop will entail fewer costs, you won't be taking that big of a risk as opposed to opening your own physical store right from the get-go.

For some businesses, they can even start an online presence before having the actual product. You can do this by building brand awareness and expanding your brand image online. Some businesses rely on building a relationship with customers online via shared experiences. They're exceptionally good at creating a connection with their users via narratives told in prose, in photos, and in other interactive methods.

Before you go live with a store of your own, an online sales channel will help you see who your target market truly is. You can get lots of valuable feedback and immediate responses from target consumers, as well as gauge the demand for your second-hand clothes before you go out and buy more inventory.

How to Set Up an Online Store

We already talked about the different sales channels you can sell your merchandise online. Often, you simply need to create an account and register. Sign in when you're ready, and start selling! Of course, with online shops, the pictures always catch the customer's eye above all else, so it's crucial that you get the best shots to market your product.

I'll dive deeper on how to take the best shots online in the later chapters of this book, but for now, all you need to know is that you should have a clear and uncluttered background when you're taking photos. You can also do cool flatlays for Instagram, and don't forget to use natural light!

Wood hangers can class up an outfit better than plastic and metal hangers. Also, you should keep the image as close to the original as possible, even if you decide to use some form of editing software after every shoot. Having a customer say he or she was duped by your photo (you don't want a customer to say the photo is different from the real thing!) is just the worst comment to receive.

Take photos of an item's front, back, and a close-up shot. Be honest and take photos of any flaws your second-hand item may have. If it's a branded item, you can take a close-up photo of the label at the back. Then, when you're satisfied with your shots, it's time to work on your descriptions.

A fabulous description should have a killer title. Don't litter it with keywords just to try to rank well on search engines. Instead, add the most important information about the item. Indicate the brand and the size clearly as well.

In the description, make sure you tell a good story if the clothing item has an interesting history. If not, just include all of the necessary information and add a personal touch— with used clothing, it's always nice to share tidbits about where the piece came from with your customers. Include color, material, flaws, and a size chart if you have one.

Be responsive with inquiries, and don't forget to factor in shipping costs in your retail price.

Getting Physical

Retail clothing stores have been around since forever, and for good reason. Physical shops provide an undeniable user experience for customers. Shopping for clothes tend to be more enjoyable for most customers when done physically in an actual store—there's just something glam and fab about browsing through the shelves and trying on clothes in your favorite clothing store.

An online store can't have the same kind of experience a physical store has for customers. Sometimes, clothes have to be seen and touched physically—this is something that customers can't experience with buying online clothes. Having the luxury of trying on the clothes themselves before making a purchase is a huge deal.

With online shops, customers can't be entirely sure if everything is legitimate or if it's all just one big scam. There are also added costs when it comes to shipping and returns. With a physical shop, customers can easily return items they're not satisfied with. They can also be a hundred percent sure that the store is legit—they're in it, after all.

It's easier to build customer trust and to ensure them that you are running a legitimate business, what with your official business license and receipts. You can also easily attract customers to your store simply by having a storefront—in online shops, you have to be able to make customers aware that you actually exist in the sea of shops on the Internet.

Physical stores also provide customers with the luxury of face-to-face staff communication. The staff at the shop can easily address any concerns that the customer may have right then and there. Issues are easily escalated, if any, to management. The customer can also negotiate and haggle with your shop employees directly if you allow negotiable price tags.

That said, you will need to factor in staffing to your start-up costs if you're going for a physical shop. Aside from the rental rate (which can be pretty hefty in itself), you have to find the perfect location for your store to thrive in your community. You also need to invest in a good point-of-sale system to keep everything in check.

Benefits of a Physical Shop

Brick-and-mortar stores offer the ultimate convenience for shoppers. In physical stores, customers can try out and buy the clothes they want, and immediately get to take them home. They won't have to wait for the delivery time before they can enjoy their favorite pieces.

Being able to check the fit of the clothes is probably the Number One advantage that physical shops have over online ones. With online stores, buyers have to take the risk of their purchases not being the right fit, or of items not having the same shade or color they want. There can be subtle differences in color when it comes to a person's computer monitor or smartphone screen as opposed to seeing the real thing.

Fabric is also a big deal. For consumers who have the luxury of trying on the clothes before purchasing, they get to experience the actual feel of the clothes on their skin. It's just not the same as in online shops, where customers have to rely on product descriptions to see what an item is made of.

With that said, all of these advantages for customers also convert into advantages for sellers. If customers find it easier, more convenient, and more enjoyable to shop in your store, then that immediately converts to sales for you.

When a customer is already inside your physical store, it's also easier for them to buy something as opposed to when they're just browsing through websites online. They feel no obligation to buy anything when they're just swiping up and down on a smartphone.

On the other hand, if they're already inside your physical store, most customers will feel a greater need or a temptation to buy something—they're more likely not going to leave without having at least tried something on. And when customers test out the merchandise, the likelihood that they'll buy something skyrockets as well.

When you have well-trained salespeople inside your store, they will be able to tip the scales greatly in your favor. Customers can easily seek them out if they have any concerns. Your store staff can also assist them with finding alternatives right off the bat in case they don't find what they're looking for. This helps you recover sales that otherwise would have been lost.

If a customer can't find what he or she is looking for in an online shop, your website will have a harder time looking for something similar you can offer to them. Inside a physical store, however, your staff can easily sway your customers to buy something else, or buy something more.

The store itself is an advertisement. As long as your signage is in good shape, you have adequate lighting, and you make your store look like a homey and inviting place to hang out in, you can easily attract buyers any time.

With a physical store, you also have more control over bestsellers and not-so-bestsellers. Your store arrangement and shelving alone can direct customers to the sections you want them to pay particular attention to. For instance, bestsellers can be right up there in front, or at the display window. If you want to push something that doesn't sell as quickly, you can easily switch the displays around so that they become more prominent and easily spotted.

Physical stores also allow you to add items to the counter. These "checkout" items are often impulse buys that you can attract customers with as they're paying for their products. Normally, these can be spur-of-the-moment accessories, add-ons, and other what-have-yous that customers can easily snatch up and include in their purchases for the day.

Customers get instant gratification in a physical store as opposed to online shops. There's just something undeniably feel-good about shopping in an actual store. Plus, a physical store provides a more secure feeling for customers when they're paying at the counter. They won't have to provide their credit card details and other personal data when checking out, and there's also no chance of having a checkout error due to faulty Internet connections.

Everything from store decor to the ambient music in the background can influence a customer to make a purchase in your physical shop. Having sociable staff and fantastic lighting, as well as a lounge area where people can hang out or companions can wait, all add to the enjoyment level that people can have in your store.

Plus, in a physical shop, you can even host small events from time to time to engage with your customers more. You can hold craft days, OOTD mini-fashion shows, collections launches with lively music, and other gimmicks that can attract random passersby to your store.

Finally, physical stores just have that physical touch. If you train your staff to provide the best customer service, or you train them to make sure that every buyer leaves the shop feeling good about themselves and their purchases, you'll be able to build customer loyalty and create a repeat customer base easily.

It's all about building relationships with actual human beings instead of links and images on a screen. There's nothing appealing about a faceless experience online, whereas a physical store can make customers feel like they are part of an actual human community with the same likes and tastes.

How to Set Up a Physical Store

We've already established the basics of what you need for your shop, and what's left is probably the first thing you need to do first before you open your store—find a good location. A strategic business location for a second-hand clothing shop may be more suitable in lower class suburbs rather than high-end neighborhoods. Reduced rates are important, so make sure you get the word out to those within your proximity.

When you have a potential location, more than the rental rates (they should be reasonable, of course), you need to do market surveys as part of your feasibility study. You should consider the accessibility of the shop (it doesn't do well to make customers suffer through a grueling commute just to get to your shop!), the number of other second-hand clothing shops in the area, and the purchasing power of the local residents. Take note of the laws and regulations for businesses in the community, as well as the statistics and demographics in the area. Be aware of the parking situation, as well as the traffic and the security.

Now, do you buy, or do you rent/lease? It will all depend on your purchasing power, but the key thing to remember is that the terms should always be favorable to you. As for your staff, you should have a store manager, sales staff, and a rider for deliveries. You might also want to have a purchasing manager and an accountant as your business grows.

Business Housekeeping

Running a business, whether online or offline, requires a great deal of preparation, and part of that preparation is the legal stuff and all the paperwork that comes with it. You need to know how to pick a legal structure, how to open a bank account, how to get enough funding, and how to get a business license, and so on.

You need to know about the best practices that go with branding and creating a logo, as well as how to keep a good image for your chosen brand. Then, you need to know how to actually set up your store! All of these things may seem tiring and mundane, but they're absolutely necessary to help you hit the ground running. Don't worry—I'll be here to guide you every step of the way.

All the Legal Things

How do you want to run your business? Do you know which business model you want to use for your used clothing venture? For instance, sole proprietorship means that you are the sole owner. All liabilities rest solely on your hands. Normally, for a start-up used clothing venture, this is the simplest and most ideal choice. It doesn't require that much paperwork, nor do you need a great deal of capital just to get up and running.

Still, if you want to be able to open up shops across plenty of cities and states, then perhaps a limited liability company is your best bet. This way, you are protected against personal liabilities that may happen during the course of you running your business. Just in case something takes a turn for the worst, your personal fund and your own assets won't be dragged down into the mud. Only the funds that you invested in your business will get affected.

In the United States, it's best to have some form of insurance policy as you get your business off the ground. There's general insurance, health insurance, liability insurance, and—if you will be hiring staff for your physical shop—workers compensation. It's also a good idea to have some form of intellectual property protection or trademark, especially if you plan on expanding your brand to launch your own line somewhere down the road. You can also protect your brand name and your logo while you're at it!

While you don't really need any form of professional certification to be able to run a used clothing business, you do need some legal paperwork to make sure you don't get shut down by the government. You will need a business license, a business and liability insurance, a building license, your operating agreement for a limited liability company, your franchise or trademark license, your tax payer's ID, and a fire certificate. If you will be conducting all of your affairs online, you will need contract documents between shipping partners, as well as your online terms of use. It's also important to have an online privacy policy document for your customers.

The beautiful thing about opening a second-hand clothing store is that you don't really need to take a huge chunk out of your savings just so you can acquire the target inventory that you need. Like we previously discussed, you can easily source second-hand clothes in lots of places, both with fees and free of charge. But if you really need more money to set things up (perhaps for your rental rates and the construction of your physical store, if you're building one), you can ask well-meaning family and friends to help you out with the financing.

If you're planning on bringing in some investors (even if they're someone you know personally), it's always a good idea to draft a solid business plan just so the investors know what they're getting themselves (and their hard-earned money) into. A good business plan will help you attract investors as well as convince financial institutions that you are serious enough and well-prepared enough so that they can grant you some financial aid.

The policies and requirements on loans will depend on your preferred bank, but having a solid business plan will still tip the scales in your favor so that you can get approved for a loan much faster.

Branding and Logo Design

One of the biggest things that can make or break a business is the logo design. A really good one can attract and keep customers, while a poorly designed one can do the exact opposite. Your brand's logo must be able to communicate clearly and effectively your business image and message while helping you establish rapport with your target market.

Big businesses spend huge chunks of their budget just to have a professional graphic designer create the perfect logo, and for good reason. While you likely won't have enough dough to hire a super professional designer for your logo (I know I didn't when I was first starting out), it's still a good idea to see if you can dip into your funds a little bit to hire someone to get it done.

There are different rates for artists, but here's something you should always remember: designers charge their rates for a reason, and you should never try to haggle their prices down to unreasonable rates. Have some respect for their craft—after all, they'll design a logo that should wow not just you as their client but all of your potential customers down the road.

With that said, deciding which visual tool to use to reach out to your customers is a big deal when establishing your brand identity. If you want to DIY your own logo (which I don't recommend, unless you're a graphic designer yourself), here are just some of the best practices you should at least try to incorporate into your logo design:

Know your brand inside and out.

Think of it this way: how will you convey to a designer (or to yourself, from your brain onto pen and paper) what you want your brand to be if you haven't figured it out yet yourself? Be sure that you at least have some insight into the brand you want to create. Remember that you are appealing to a certain target market, while at the same time, you want to make sure that everything that your brand stands for must be communicated into the design.

What is your brand ideology? What are your business aspirations? Are you perhaps an eco-warrior? Or do you fancy something hipper and out-of-this-world for your used clothing store? All of these elements should be reflected in the banners, social media posts, packaging, business card, website design, and so on.

Make a good impression.

Your logo will be representing your business in more ways than one, so it's important that every color used reflects the nature of your shop. The images should align with your brand's values, as well as effectively portray what it is you sell (the clothes, of course). This type of brand identity helps keep you ahead in the game or stand out from your other competitors in the market.

The logo will immediately convey a message to your customers without a single word. You're not always going to be around to explain or engage with your users, so you need to make sure that your logo is at its best. It should not only make a lasting impression on your customers, but it should also be simple and easy enough to remember that it embeds an image into the users' minds in an instant.

Of course, you shouldn't forget to make your logo as unique as possible—you wouldn't want to be associated with other brands out there (or worse, get associated with a brand that has a less-than-favorable reputation in the market). You wouldn't want to be mistaken for someone else, either! You want to make a name for yourself, so imitating brands and logo lookalikes are a huge no-no. Don't try to imitate a well-known brand in hopes of riding on that brand's fame and association with its target market. They may say that imitation is the best form of flattery, but you're never going to arrive anywhere with that kind of cheap imitation.

Be mindful of your colors.

I already mentioned this earlier, but it's important enough to repeat—make those colors work to your advantage. People have different associations with color, the basic ones being red as passion and excitement and blue as peace and calm. Whatever color you decide to use, make sure that it aligns with your brand vision. This is precisely why knowing your brand inside and out is crucial when designing your logo. What kind of feelings do you want to evoke in your customers when they see your logo?

To really grab your target market's attention, use bright colors and the right combination. There is a science to color combination (color theory has always been a fascinating way of reaching out to your customers with a single glance). You should either use complementary colors or analogous colors. The former refers to hues that are exactly opposite from each other on the color wheel, while the latter refers to those that are adjacent with each other and therefore less contrasting.

Use the right fonts.

Just like color theory, fonts can also make or break your logo. It's a completely different beast altogether, with different typefaces that refer to different uses. Whimsical and more playful styles will have handwritten typefaces, while those that aim for a more serious approach will likely use a straightforward serif or sans serif font.

You also have the option of having a font customized, but if you don't have that luxury, there are plenty of fonts online you can choose from. Try to mix and match with your logo to see which one looks and feels best.

The typeface of your logo will also be instrumental in helping you convey the right message, so try to avoid fonts that are too gimmicky. Not only will this look unprofessional, but it might also not be too legible from afar. Remember: if you're opening up a physical shop, that logo font will be front and center on your banner, so you want to make sure people can actually read what your shop's name is.

Keep it simple and scalable.

Nobody likes a messy logo that looks like the owner tried to cram everything in there at the last minute. Simple logo designs are best, and they look loads more professional. Generally, there should only be one or two colors, as well as fonts and other elements in the logo. Other extra details will just prove to be distracting for customers, and they may end up sending mixed signals you don't really want to portray.

Keeping the logo simple will also make it more memorable. Plus, it'll also be easier to print or recreate in any marketing material you might have. This is where scalability comes in. Because it will be featured in a variety of advertisements, it should be adjustable for different uses from small handouts to big billboards.

This is also why it's important to only have minimal elements in your logo. Having too many things crammed in there will make it illegible when it's printed on smaller surfaces. Not every detail may translate well into smaller prints, so keeping it simple goes hand-in-hand with scalability.

Add a colorless version.

I know I talked a lot about color and how important it is, but sometimes, a certain situation will require you to have your logo presented in simple grayscale or black and white. This can happen when it's printed on faxed documents, stationery, or newspaper ads. You need to make sure that even when it's stripped to the bare minimum, your logo can still stand on its own and convey the message you want to convey.

Find what sets you apart, and embed it in your brand.

What is your company's purpose? What is the goal you want your brand to achieve? What is your unique selling point (USP), and how do you show this to your customers in a single glance? It's definitely not easy to figure all of this out and incorporate them into your logo design, but if you do your research or get inspiration from other brands out there, you'll get there.

Don't be afraid to experiment with different looks—designing your logo isn't something you can get done overnight! See what works and what doesn't, and don't be afraid to start over. It's the most important first step to establishing your brand identity, so it's understandable that it needs a lot of time and effort.

Inventory Management

Good inventory management can not only help you start your business, but it can also help you keep it going. If you don't invest in the right kind of inventory management system, sales and records can be an absolute nightmare—just imagine having to sort through piles and piles of clothes without any kind of organization whatsoever!

While you may think that an ordinary cash box or cash register can already be considered a sales system on its own, manually inputting everything into a spreadsheet just doesn't cut it anymore these days. You need to be able to somehow operate your inventory, point of sale, and price seamlessly via a desktop or a mobile device.

Retail management should be organized from the get-go so that you won't end up with random files and missing documents or sales in the long run. You can invest in technology systems that are scalable for your convenience, but if you don't want to have too many out-of-pocket expenses, you can purchase scanners, merchandise tags, and pricing equipment and integrate them instead.

With an integrated point-of-sale (POS) system, you can log the styles and sizes for all of your merchandise. Include a UPC barcode for scanning if you have a physical shop. This will not only help you check inventory in an instant, but it will also make it easier for your employees to process returns at the register.

When you're organizing your items inside the shop, make sure that they are folded or hung and arranged according to size and style. Your stock room should be similarly organized so that your employees won't have to rummage around in there for the longest time just to find the right size that a customer is looking for. Remember: it pays to be quick and efficient, as long wait times can affect customer experience negatively.

Make sure that you put clear and easy-to-spot labels on each item packaging in the stockroom, and don't interchange them! This will not only provide a better working experience for your employees, but it will also provide a better shopping experience for your loyal customers.

Whenever you receive any new inventory, create a systematic way of organizing receipts. Deal with shipments in a way that doesn't disrupt your already existing inventory counts. Keep enclosed manifests that come with merchandise deliveries, and double check all of the details listed to ensure that the right items are being delivered as indicated.

Count the items physically when you can. Have your own checklist where you can cross reference the delivery. This way, you can immediately notify your supplier for any shipping mishaps, replacements, or refunds.

If you can afford it, make sure you invest in electronic loss prevention stickers or tags. These prove to be good deterrents for thieves in your store; plus, it also forces your staff to handle your merchandise with care.

When your store closes, make it a habit to check the inventory physically at least once every month. Print out a copy of your inventory from your automatic POS, and cross reference what you actually have inside your store and see if the numbers match. Good fashion inventory management helps you avoid having out-of-stock items or overselling to customers when you no longer have the item. It helps keep your storage space efficient, and saves time and effort both for your employees and your customers.

If you keep stock-outs to a minimum, you effectively increase customer satisfaction for the long haul. Customers will react favorably to your brand more, and you also prevent the risk of them looking for that same item somewhere else if they can't find it in your shop. It builds customer trust, which is key when building loyalty and a strong brand word-of-mouth.

With good inventory management, you maintain a healthy cash flow that's not tied up in labor hours and managing inventory. You reduce storage costs and insurance costs, as well as reduce the chances of lost items, theft, or damaged goods.

Manually logging your inventory can be prone to human error, and it's not too scalable when you do decide to branch out and expand. The spreadsheet method is more feasible than listing things down on pen and paper, but this will only be viable while your business is still in its budding first stages.

It's important to have a master list of everything (for instance, using Google Sheets is better than having multiple files of the same Excel spreadsheet in different computers).

This way, there's only a singular source of everything that you actually have, and you can control who gets to view or edit the file, as necessary. This is a good way to collaborate with employees, partners, and managers as well.

If you can afford it, and if your business has grown big enough, you can invest in mobile-based apparel inventory management tools to reduce errors as much as possible. You can take photos of an item and upload all kinds of information for each merch, as well as integrate everything with a mobile scanner to make sure everything lines up the way they should.

An electronic system like this can also be exported into a spreadsheet report should you need one. As your business gets bigger and better (let's certainly hope so!), you can move on to an Enterprise Resource Planning (ERP) Tool that also includes a Warehouse Management System (WMS) Integration. This will be full automation for your inventory, preventing costly oversights and inaccuracies, as well as improving overall shipping methods and schedules.

Sales Policies

With good inventory management come good sales policies that will help you get organized when it comes to fulfilling customer orders. While selling used clothes may seem simple enough, there are tons of things to consider behind the scenes to make sure you stay afloat for years and years to come. Keep your business thriving with the right policies that will give you an edge over others in the market.

In-store policies

When you're operating a physical store you need to make sure that all of your employees are following proper guidelines. If you have multiple staff, make sure that each person has his own task and that every task has a specific schedule. This not only ups the ante when it comes to organization and division of labor, but it also makes sure that accountability is on-point.

Rather than operate by the seat of your pants, have a specific set of work rules even before you open up your store. Make sure that you iron out the details now so that any decision-making that needs to be done later on will be easier and quicker to do.

Store hours

Business hours and store hours are two very different things in retail. During business hours, this is when you get internal tasks done like tagging, preparing merchandise, receiving items, freshening up your displays, cleaning shelves, organizing clothes, folding and hanging items, organizing storage, counting the cash in your register, checking new deliveries, ordering new supplies, returning damaged products, processing returns and refunds, answering customer queries, checking markdowns, and so much more. These all happen behind the scenes and may seem secondary to the actual selling, but they make up the backbone of your day-to-day business operations, and if you don't get them organized and done the right way, you're simply setting your business up for failure.

Now, you normally can't accomplish these tasks during store hours. Store hours are the actual hours of operation for your shop. This is when you interact with walk-in customers and do the actual selling—both these types of hours are crucial when you're running your second-hand clothing store.

To make sure you stay sane all throughout the process, learn to define your personal limits. Set realistic goals and hours to accomplish them in. You don't have to get every single thing done in just a single day, and you don't have to do everything by yourself, either. Draft a planned schedule and stick to it as much as you can, or else you might end up picking up the slack from previous weeks, adding up to a huge pile of backlogs as the months go by.

For instance, ask yourself the following questions:

- Do you have extended hours during holidays?

- Are your store hours fixed, or do they vary on weekends?

- Do you have operating hours for customer service channels?

- Do you have operating hours online?

Policies on credit

Nowadays, you just can't get by without accepting credit cards from customers anymore as a business. It's important to sign up for MasterCard, American Express, or Visa—this will normally entail a small percentage to let your bank handle the credit details. You should have detailed credit policies so that your customers know which modes of payment you can accept, both online and in physical stores.

For instance, ask yourself the following questions:

- What currencies do you accept?

- Do accept check payments?

- Do you allow credit extensions?

- What is your markup?

- Do you offer discounts on wholesale purchases?

- Do you have employee perks?

Policies on returns and exchanges

Not every single customer purchase will go smoothly. A huge part of good customer service is how you handle returns, exchanges, and refunds. You should decide on how you want to accept them, and if you have limits when it comes to the timeframe (some businesses offer 7-day returns, 30-day returns, and so on). You normally want customers to return items with the tags and original packaging still intact.

You should also figure out if you want to offer gift-wrapping on special occasions, alterations for bottoms, special orders, free deliveries, and so on. All of these can add to a customer's overall shopping experience, and will determine if they'll give you a good score when it comes to excellent customer service.

For instance, ask yourself the following questions:

- Do you need proof of purchase for refunds?

- Do you have a return form?

- Do you accept special orders with deposits?

- What are your countermeasures for customers who fail to pick up special orders or alterations?

Security policies

Believe it or not, billions of dollars are lost each year due to crimes. You can reduce the chances of getting robbed if you keep your cash on hand at a minimum, as well as schedule different times for bank deposits. You should keep a safe secured inside the store, be on the lookout for suspicious characters.

It's always best to be safe than sorry. Cooperate with the local police, and give your staff basic training on what to do in case of a robbery. You should also provide training on what to do in case of power failures and other emergencies.

Policies on housekeeping

Cleanliness is extremely important both inside your physical store and inside your office if you have one. Set standards for cleanliness and create a checklist for your employees so that they can maintain a well-kept shop and in turn entice more customers into the store. It's always more pleasant to shop in a store that's in tip-top shape rather than in one that's filthy and disorganized.

Recording your policies

You should neatly document each policy in a manual or handbook for your employees. Have several copies (both soft copies and hard copies) and distribute as needed. Have a spare copy by the cash register for quick reference as well. Be strict enough to enforce them, but flexible enough to revise them when needed.

Sell, Sell, Sell

If it feels like there's a lot of stuff you need to take in right now, bear with me! I promise it'll all be worth it once your second-hand shop is up and running. Believe me—I understand. I was in the same position after losing Gran, and while at first I thought I could just go ahead and sell (it should be as simple as trading clothes for money, right?), it ended up getting more complicated the more I got into it.

Here's the thing: if you're just looking to get rid of extra clutter around the house and make a few bucks while doing it, you might be able to get away with not organizing your whole system. But if you're planning on doing this for the long haul, you need to do everything you can to be as prepared as possible.

A huge number of start-ups fail because of poor planning (or a significant lack of it), so don't fall into that same trap. Being as prepared as you possibly can—and taking all factors into account—will significantly increase your chances of success when it comes to actually selling, selling, selling.

Equipment and Advertising

For physical used clothing shops, you will need dressing rooms, hangers, display racks, shelves, showcases, mirrors, mannequins, and your cash register. You need to be able to set aside a chunk of your budget for these necessities. Aim for the most value so that all of your acquisitions are cost-efficient.

Your store layout furnishings must speak to the customer. When you invest in your racks and display cases, you need to take in to consideration the customer's shopping experience as well as your brand colors and the atmosphere you want to give off. Even something as seemingly insignificant as your overhead background music will contribute greatly to the ambiance or the vibe of your shop.

Your theme aesthetics as well as the material of your racks are all important. For instance, custom-made wooden furniture gives off a classier and more high-end vibe than low-cost gondola shelves. Make sure that the clothes you're selling are in tune with the overall feel of the shop.

As for your display materials, you need your logo to be front and center, prominently advertising your shop and making you stand out. This is especially important if you are located in an area with high foot traffic—you want to make sure that all of those people passing by your shop don't go to waste.

Here are just a few marketing ideas and strategies you can look into to be proactive in your enterprise:

Direct Marketing

You can do direct marketing via door-to-door sales. Direct marketing channels may also include email, direct mail, or

SMS. These methods allow you to engage with your customer directly, increasing brand loyalty in the process. Also, with direct marketing, you are able to track your progress relatively easily because you can monitor the results directly. You can analyze the results of any direct marketing campaign and identify areas for improvement. You can accentuate any strengths and continuously tweak your campaigns to improve.

With direct marketing, you also have the pleasure of personalizing your marketing efforts for your target market. You can base your campaign on actual experiences, as well as employ customer segmentation and data profiling techniques to further get to know your customer on a face-to-face level.

This way, you will also be able to reduce any counter-moves made by your competitors. Unlike with TV ads and internet advertising, direct marketing addresses your customer personally, and your campaign speaks to them in a more intimate way.

Of course, direct marketing techniques have a very limited reach. Compared to mass broadcast ads like TV or radio, you can only really reach out to the customer in a restrictive space. Some customers are also very picky when it comes to whom they allow into their inboxes, so you have to have that option for them to opt into your newsletters or subscriptions to prevent any breach of privacy.

Online marketing

You can also do online marketing via your social media channels and your official website or blog. Internet marketing is a low-cost promotion strategy that eliminates the need for any physical capital. You can easily reach a global market with online marketing, especially if you have your own website on a good host server (and a good domain name). Your used clothing store will effectively reach users all over the world with just a click of a link, and you're not limited to a specific geographical area.

If you have good keywords in your website or blog, customers will also be able to find you easily. You don't even have to look for them—they'll end up looking for you if you have a good search engine ranking. It's essentially advertising that's open 24/7, with convenient payment options and an always-open shop.

You can also make some extra money from affiliate marketing. For example, websites and blogs often have Amazon affiliates, where owners of these websites earn a little bit of extra money whenever someone clicks on a link to a product that directs them back to the Amazon website. This passive income is a nice little icing on the cake when you're marketing your shop online.

Unfortunately, online marketing can sometimes be prone to trust issues. There are plenty of scam ads and digital malware related to some unsolicited banners. You will also have the biggest set of competitors as essentially, anyone can click on something else entirely while they're on the Internet. With all of the different voices vying for a customer's attention easily accessible and available online, it can be difficult to stand out from the crowd. Search engine rankings alone always have changing algorithms that can be hard to crack without a dedicated SEO manager.

Traditional advertising

By the word "traditional" alone, you can already tell what this is: print, broadcast, and other commercials. This includes television and radio, as well as magazines, billboards, newspapers, brochures, and flyers. It's been around for the longest time, which just goes to show you how effective these methods are.

Traditional marketing campaigns have proven effective time and time again, so you definitely won't have a hard time figuring out how to do them, as you can use past examples to pattern yours after. There are tons of research papers and analyses that have been conducted on traditional advertising for varying target markets.

Traditional techniques also have an immensely wider reach. They don't target individuals specifically, so you can also reach would-be customers you didn't even know about. Of course, the same pro can also be a con, as it's definitely not as personal as direct marketing. It doesn't have that personalized touch that some customers look for in a brand.

Trad efforts target groups rather than individuals. It's more of a "quantity over quality" reach, so while you might reach tons and tons of people, not all of them will be relevant customers who will actually convert those ads into sales.

Plenty of print versions of ads are now moving to online channels as well. As such, print ads are less effective for younger markets and the millennial demographic. These ads more predictable by virtue of being traditional, and people can easily skip over commercials and ignore billboards if they wanted to. This will really depend on the type of used clothing you're selling—if your target market is on the younger side, then print ads probably won't be your best bet.

Other methods

There are plenty of other methods you can use to get your message across and reach your customers wherever they may be. You can sponsor TV shows and radio programs, or you can engage in referral marketing. Here, you can give bonus incentives to customers who refer your site or brand to someone else. You can also participate in various road shows within your local community. This should be near your physical shop in your area.

You can hire the services of an agent or a sales rep to advertise your brand for you. You can list yourself in directories, both in print and online. Some bloggers and online influencers can market your brand for exposure in exchange for various goods or monetary compensation. You can also create your very own blog where you can give value to customers by posting about informational aspects of clothes. This can be anything from how to care for old clothes and fabric to how to repair basic sewing mishaps.

Pricing Guide

How do you price your items? Aside from used clothing, you can also sell accessories that go with them, like hats, bags, purses, or even shoes. You can always branch out just like with any other item in the retail industry, but the thing about second-hand clothing is that the pricing is usually the more challenging aspect of selling. You have to make sure that you price the items just right, and that the price tags are justified by the quality and the rarity of the item.

For instance, if a piece is really pretty but has a bunch of holes in it, you can't possibly sell it for a higher price. The condition of your wares will likely dictate the price, but so can how rare it can be, especially if it's vintage. You might also be able to place a higher price tag on items that have an interesting history, like if they were owned by someone famous or if they were used in some historically significant way.

On the other end of the spectrum, while people often shop for used clothes in order to save up on costs, pricing your items too low can give off the impression that the clothes don't have any value. It can be difficult to find that sweet spot, that right balance between being too extravagant and being too cheap. To help you get started, you should at least do your research.

The market is always a good place to start. It's going to dictate how much you should price your item, and the longer you hang around the second-hand clothing industry, the better your grasp of the prices will be. The most seasoned experts immediately know how to price an item just by looking at it, but you don't have to have that kind of guru expertise—you can do due diligence and scour markets, bazaars, and other used clothing stores (online or physical) to see how much an item is worth.

From outrageous to downright silly, prices can make or break customer loyalty and perception. You wouldn't want to be caught dead selling the exact same thing for a marginally higher price than a competitor, or it just leaves a poor taste in the customer's mouth. It reduces word-of-mouth referral too.

Now, sellers will each have their own approach to pricing, but there are a few tools you can use to determine base prices, at the very least. On Grailed, you can check the online marketplace's price comparison feature to learn more about similar items. It's also important to be open to negotiations.

One effective strategy you can use is to justify your pricing with good, high-quality shipping. Branded packaging can really raise the bar and set you up higher than your competitors, even if they may be selling something similar for a lower price.

Aside from branded packaging, you can also use reusable ones since sustainability is the name of the game right now. Being an eco-warrior is also a huge plus for your brand, as more like-minded individuals will flock to your brand because of that advocacy. You can use packaging that can be folded or repurposed as a variety of things like magazine holders, cardboard stands, fun garden ornaments, or even Mason jar trinkets. These things help unleash your customer's creativity while they're at home too!

For example, there are so many ways you can repurpose a Pringles can, with users posting how-to blogs on how to turn them into kitchen holders and even speakers. It's a brilliant and non-traditional way to get advertised by your own customers—the more they post about blogs on how to creatively reuse your packaging, the more you get free advertising and the more other people become aware of your brand. It's definitely a win-win situation!

Of course, you shouldn't forget to slip your label, logo, or business card in there for full low-key advertising effect.

As for the logistics of shipping, you can also justify your pricing with priority shipments as well as making sure that there are no delays and extra hidden fees. Make sure that you secure your packages properly with sealed waterproof bags and bubble wrap if needed.

You can also offer discounted prices for bulk orders. Don't be closed off to negotiations, especially if you're selling at bazaars and fairs. People love a good bargain, and even just the tiniest drop in price will leave your customers satisfied. Bear in mind that if you do decide to participate in a garage sale, you have to set the lowest prices because that's just what a garage sale is, by nature.

You can also bundle clothing items that you think go best together, or you can pair the not-so-popular ones with the bestselling ones in order to push out some of that inventory. You can charge a bundle price as well—this way, it's not going to be easy for your customers to compare your prices and items with your competitors.

When you're bundling, you can also bundle by fashion brand. If you have bigger bundles, your buyer likely won't be trying every single thing on first, so make sure that you price it properly. Know what the current retail price is. Don't be afraid to browse the websites or shops of those big brands (if they still carry the item) just to do some research.

On an average, you can probably set the resale price at approximately half the original cost provided that the condition is still fairly new. Designer goods and antique jewelry will have different prices, as will items that have sentimental value.

Selling Hacks for the Future Clothing Guru

How do you make the best listings on online selling channels and apps? How do you make sure you get noticed in the marketplace? How do you post the best photos out there, and what in the world is Amazon FBA?

From online best practices to how to organize your in-store display at a physical shop, this section details all the insider tips you need to know to become the next used clothing guru.

I've got just the thing!

Online Tips and Tricks

The most important things you need to work on with online shops are your photos. You have to be able to showcase your items clearly and in an appealing manner. You can use models or a mannequin, as long as all of the styles are consistent.

Now, when I say styles, this doesn't just mean you need to have either models or mannequins. Style also encompasses constant angles, constant lighting, and a constant vibe or feel to your photos. A lot of business owners use filters (and there are limitless options for apps you can use out there to add filters to your photos), but if you really want to look professional, you should begin with good well-lighted shots. Don't make the amateur mistake of thinking that a good filter can hide a really bad shot. Filters can only enhance what's already there, and what's already there should be a really well-taken photo.

You just can't get any more amateurish than fuzzy shots that look like they were haphazardly taken with a random camera phone. It's important to invest in a decent DSLR camera, or at the very least, a high-end smartphone model with top-notch camera specs. They always say that a picture is worth a thousand words, and with selling second-hand clothes online, this adage can't be any truer.

Remember—if you don't feel like you would buy something based on its photo, chances are that your customers will feel the same way.

Part of the appeal of online shopping for consumers is the convenience of having everything they need and want at their fingertips. It should also be an enjoyable experience for the customer as they're browsing through your wares in your shop, and they can't enjoy looking at your clothes if the photos are shoddy. Poorly taken photos also give customers the illusion that your shop isn't trustworthy, and that you're not professional enough to at least have some decent shots. It's all about presentation, and being able to showcase beautiful images shows that your wares are actually worth a click.

With that said, here are just some of the most important things I learned as I was going through this whole journey myself:

Invest in a good camera, even if it's from a smartphone.

If you already own a high-end DSLR or you know someone who can lend you theirs, then by all means, go for it. But if you're like me as I was starting out, chances are that you won't have that kind of hi-tech equipment readily available on hand.

Nowadays, flagship models of smartphones have all kinds of fancy tools to help you get started on your journey to photographing your clothes. Even the most basic settings already look stunning—you can also mostly customize the settings if you're privy to the techie stuff, or you can just set everything to auto and let your phone decide the best way to do the shoot. Smartphones are smart enough to know the kind of lighting you're shooting in most of the time.

Invest in a tripod to keep those wobbly shots at bay.

If you think you can get away with propping your smartphone against something to take the perfect shot, you're absolutely wrong (don't feel bad about it—I did the same thing before all this). Not only is this incredibly unstable, it also won't make your shots consistent. You can't possibly be able to prop your phone in exactly the same position throughout your whole business venture.

These inconsistencies may be seemingly insignificant, but the notable differences will be obvious once all of your photos are lined up against each other in grids on the online channel. It will be incredibly challenging to standardize everything if your camera source isn't consistent.

This is where the tripod comes in. You don't need anything too fancy—in fact, there are plenty of affordable and value-for-money tripods out there for all kinds of phones. You don't need the heavy duty industrial-sized models just to get the perfect shot from your phone.

When you're picking the right one for you, you can either choose traditional or flexible tripods. A traditional tripod is often extendable with a solid stand, while a flexible tripod can be shorter but has a flexible mount with adjustable legs. This is especially useful if you're not going to be shooting from a flat surface, and you need to angle your camera somewhere uneven.

You should also take into consideration how well the tripod grips your smartphone. You wouldn't want to be taking the perfect shot only to have your phone fall to the floor in the middle of it (or worse, run the risk of damaging your smartphone).

Use natural light.

Good lighting can make a world of difference when you want to make the subject of your photo look as appealing as it can be. Buyers make their purchasing decisions by inspecting an item thoroughly, and since they can't do that in person with an online shop, the best thing you can do is to simulate being able to see the item in person with good photos taken in natural lighting.

Lighting arrangements might be a challenge to set up, so it's important to have a specific corner or area in your home or office where the sunlight hits best. You should also factor in the time of day when shooting, as the sun's varying positions overhead can drastically change the lighting and shadows of a shot.

It's also important to remember that sunlight casts a softer light on any subject. Your set should be able to thrive in natural light outside. With used clothing, this is especially effective if you're using models who will be wearing the actual clothes. If they're outside and under natural light, the sun brings out the best in them as well as provides a soft light that helps them look their most presentable.

If you can't use natural light, use artificial light, and use it well.

With artificial light, you can use fire, candles, and, of course, light bulbs. These are referred to commonly as "hard light", as sunlight is softer while these produce smaller light surfaces with a more focused radius. If your clothing items have specific details that you need to highlight to the customer, hard light is the best light source to use.

Of course, whether you decide to use natural light or artificial light, it's best to choose just one for every photo. If something should look sharp, natural light can soften it unnecessarily, and vice versa. You wouldn't want to confuse your customer, nor would you want to counter your own strategies to highlight product features in a single photo.

There are tons of techniques you can use to manipulate your light.

If you want to lessen the shadows caused by hard light that is cast on the product's opposite end, you can use fill light. A fill light is a different light source that's often less intense than your main light source. It is used to supplement the lighting, and can effectively counterbalance hard, natural shadows and soften them. Often, your main light will produce a shadow behind an item. To soften this, you can place a fill light that is positioned on the opposite side of your main light. Your item will sit between the two light sources and be illuminated in a better way.

You can also use a flashbulb bounce card. This is a small card that can bounce the main light back. The bounce card or reflector card reflects the light beneath your product onto the surface, effectively reducing the shadows. In a professional camera, the bounce card is usually attached to the flashbulb. The attached flashbulb in the camera lens can diffuse the light caused by the flash of the camera. With this card, a softer light is cast onto the subject, making the light shin down from above the set rather than directly straight at it. This eliminates long shadows behind your subject.

If you're using a smartphone instead of a professional camera, you won't be able to attach a flashbulb bounce card because there is no physical flash. You can DIY your card and position it opposite the main source of light. This can also be a replacement for your fill light if you don't have one—it does a fantastic job of countering the hard light form your light source that's placed in front of your merchandise.

It's important to be able to reduce the shadows that are cast onto your items, all while being able to highlight all of the qualities and features of your merch.

To highlight your product, use portrait mode or sweep.

Depending on the type of background that you use, there are different ways lights and bounce cards can go wrong. It's important to choose a background that effectively highlights your product—don't choose one over the other just because it's easier to do. Make sure that you pick a background that positively affects how you want your customers to perceive your merch.

Do you want to use a white background, or do you prefer a more dynamic, real-world background? With a clean, white backdrop, you can use a sweep. It's important to know that even the best cameras on your phone will still be able to pick up specks and blemishes against a seemingly white wall. No matter how plain you think your background is, there are still little things that you won't be able to notice with the naked eye.

With a sweep, you can ensure a better, whiter, cleaner background. A sweep is essentially a big sheet of paper that's bendable. The bottom part of the paper will act as the flat surface underneath your items. It effectively curves up into a white wall at the back of your item. Surprisingly, the curve of this sweep will not be visible on the camera's shot. This will help you emphasize the key details of your product while keeping your buyer's attention focused solely on the merchandise. It's a little bit like magic, isn't it?

When you are using a real-world background behind your items, it's important to use the portrait mode. Because real-world backdrops are dynamic, they can up the ante when it comes to how appealing a product can be. This is especially effective if a real person is modelling your merch. However, because real-world backdrops are equally as appealing to look at, it can be difficult for your buyer to focus on a single thing. You want them to focus their attention on the clothes that you are selling and not on the background.

Even the most professional cameras will still have the basic portrait mode setting. Smartphones will likely have these set automatically, and they provide the clothes that you are selling with plenty of product depth and emphasis. This setting will effectively blur the background a little bit so that the viewer's eye is instantly drawn to the context or subject of your photo. It will be clearer and more emphasized, and the background won't be competing with your products.

Take different angles.

Do not be satisfied with just a single photo for each product. Just because you think you have the perfect photo doesn't mean that you should call it a day! It's important to be able to capture what makes each item unique, appealing, and valuable to the customer. Remember—your customers will be able to look at, hold, test out, fit, and use an item in a physical store, and none of that is possible with an online one. This is exactly why you should take the best photos to make sure you simulate this experience in the best way you can.

Take as many angles as you can, as what may be obvious for a customer in a physical store may not be immediately obvious for a buyer in an online store. To be able to capture the fabric and the garment of your clothing, you need to spread the item out on a flat surface and zoom in on the details of the fabric. If the clothing is on a mannequin, the item should be contrasting in color compared to the mannequin for more emphasis. If you can, have the item modelled by an actual person as well. Take different shots—

115

one on a flat surface, one on a mannequin, and one on a person for full effect.

Having different quality photos will also ensure your buyer that you are legit, and that you're not trying to conceal anything with your merchandise. You're proving to them that you want to be as cooperative and helpful as possible, providing them with as many details as possible so that when the time does come for them to make a purchasing decision, it will be absolute and done without a single doubt.

Amazon FBA

If you've been researching about selling online for a while now, you might have come across the term "Amazon FBA" from time to time. At the very least, you know what Amazon is—it's unlikely that you've never bought or tried to buy anything from this big online marketplace. After all, Amazon has over two million people selling their wares worldwide, as almost anyone can post an item for sale on the website.

As one of the most popular ways to earn some extra cash online, Amazon has practically everything from wholesale goods to hand-crafted trinkets. If you want to make use of this incredibly powerful online sales channel, you should consider enrolling in the FBA program, where order fulfilment can be automated via the advanced shipping and fulfilment services from Amazon itself. This way, you can also tap into Amazon Prime customers.

Short for Fulfilment by Amazon, FBA basically means that whatever you sell, Amazon ships. In essence, you send your products over to the Amazon warehouses, where they keep them safe and secure. Then, whenever a buyer orders an item from your shop, Amazon takes charge of picking, packing, shipping, and tracking the order—all of these are done on your behalf. Amazon will also handle returns and refunds.

Now, while this sounds like it's all too good to be true, it all comes at a price, of course. There are storage fees and fulfilment fees you need to take into account, but along with those fees, you also get top-notch 24/7 customer service from Amazon.

You also get much-coveted access to Amazon Prime customers, who understandably spend more money on shops than regular customers. There are over 300 million active customers on Amazon—not to tap into that is just plain crazy!

When you send your products over to Amazon, they will notify you about which of their 100 warehouses across the country will store your product. They sort and store your merchandise, and in case something does get damaged,

Amazon will take responsibility and reimburse you for it. When a customer purchases your item, Amazon manages the whole transaction for you, stress-free and hassle-free. They'll also be in charge of accepting payment and updating your inventory.

Every two weeks, your sales all get totaled, and Amazon deducts any seller fees before depositing your profits into your bank account—easy-peasy.

Now, because Amazon handles the whole transaction for you, the least you can do is to really step up your game with your products and postings. To avoid more expensive storage fees, make sure that your inventory turnover is pretty quick and always in stock. Market and advertise your products (just like we discussed!) like a boss—you will have more time to do this because of Amazon's effortless logistics and shipping. You get discounted shipping rates, not to mention Prime members get to enjoy free two-day shipping, which is something that you can use to boost your sales.

With FBA, you also get virtually unlimited storage space, as Amazon's warehouses are vast. You save time and energy as they handle time-consuming returns and customer inquires and concerns for you. As an added bonus, you can also avail of the Multi-Channel Fulfilment (MCF) service which will let you use FBA even if you sell on other online sales channels like BigCommerce.

Still, storage fees can get really costly if your items sit untouched form more than half a year. You need to follow Amazon's strict guidelines when it comes to shipping your items to them, with correctly labelled items and properly entered data into Amazon's database. You will also have to factor in the sales tax, which is different for every state in America.

Now, there are also a few cons to using Amazon FBA. If you sell on Amazon, you will virtually have unlimited competitors all offering the same logistics and handling. Amazon's stores will all be your competitors, as you are all in the same big marketplace. It's important to be able to research your closest competitors to check whether or not your items stand a chance.

You can try to use services like Unicorn Smasher or AMZ Scout, where you can review estimated monthly sales as well as valuable competitor knowledge. Consider the sales rank of items, and think about using bundled listings. This helps you get an extra edge over other competitors. A buyer will definitely find a top-and-necklace combo more value-for-money than just a simple top alone. And because you are all basically using the same shipping logistics, you can make your shop stand out by adding inserts and cute packages to differentiate you from the rest.

Fantastic photos and great descriptions are a given. As for your title, don't do keyword stuffing! This will probably be shortened by Amazon anyway—plus, it makes you look super unprofessional if you just keep trying to cram all those keywords in there even if they make no sense. Aim for a clear, descriptive title that doesn't seem spammy. Go for your brand name, your product name, and then add relevant features like the color or the size. That way, you lay out all of the information without going overboard with all the keywords.

Amazon listings often have bullet points that serve as a sort of "at a glance" description of your items. Make sure that you pay special attention to these! Those first few points will be what your customers will check out first if they want more details about your clothing, so make sure you indicate all of the necessary information briefly. Include its history, its fabric, and flaws if any. Those bullet points have to answer the buyer's questions about your product at first glance.

Now, if you feel like there isn't much space for you to really get into great detail about the clothes you're selling, don't worry—if the customer is interested enough, they will scroll down further to check what else you have to say.

Here's your chance to expound on everything you briefly mentioned in the bullet points. You can provide comprehensive descriptions and add more photos (or videos!) for your clothes. You can even tell your brand story if you want to, just to make a customer feel like you're really legit and that there's a strong reputation behind your trustworthy brand.

There's also a question and answer portion further below the page. Normally, anyone can post a question and answer it, whether or not they're actual buyers. If you want to make sure that the information is accurate, you can request a friend to ask a question that you can answer yourself. This way, you can increase engagement and address the most common questions right off the bat.

As for the reviews, you really can't manipulate your way out of this one—your product and your customer service both have to be really top-notch in order to get good reviews. It's important to provide value and quality to your customers so that they'll be happy to leave a good review after purchasing your clothes.

Merchandising Tips and Tricks

If you're opening a physical store, visual merchandising should be one of your top priorities. Strategies in visual merchandising will help you decide how to present and display your products to drive sales, including everything from lighting to signage. You can get creative with your product displays and improve your sales growth, all by knowing how to arrange aspects of your physical store.

Always think of the customer.

Who is your ideal customer? By now, you should at least know who your target market is, and what elements and aesthetics will appeal to them. Create displays that appeal not to you but to your customer. Just because something looks aesthetically pleasing to you personally doesn't mean it'll have the same effect on your target market.

Use lighting to create displays that will attract them. If they're edgy when it comes to fashion choices, go for dramatic lighting or hard edges. If they're more refined and feminine, go for bright whites or pastel pinks to create the best visual elements that will elevate the customer experience based on their unique tastes and personalities.

Engage the senses.

Visual merchandising may be "visual", but that doesn't mean you should neglect all the other senses. Shopping inside your store should be an experience, and the most memorable ones are those that engage all of a person's senses. Delight the customer with the right ambient music, or use the power of scent to influence purchasing decisions.

For instance, if you sell athletic used clothes and outdoor outfits, you can use light woodsy scents to appeal to your target market. Emotions are linked to smell, and even triggered by them. Draw your buyer into an unforgettable experience by adding the right elements of smell and sound (subtly, and not overpowering!) in your shop.

It's all about subtle product placement.

The energy levels of a customer fade gradually as they move about and stay longer inside your store. To make sure that you maximize those precious first few moments inside your shop, place the trendiest and most recent bestsellers near the front of your shop. This will make sure that customers see the most interesting items first while their energy levels are high and their moods are good.

Items on sale or other low-cost clothes may be placed in the back, or perhaps near the counter as a last-minute impulse buy. You also have the option of placing discounted items in front if you're advertising a huge sale to drag the customers in.

Rotate your merchandise.

That said, don't be afraid to shake things up when it comes to product placement. Repositioning your items may depend on trial and error—if customers respond one way, then act accordingly. Rotate your product displays every few weeks. This will make sure that your displays are always fresh and exciting.

Think of it this way: if you pass by the same store over and over again and their displays remain the same each time, wouldn't it seem like the shop is boring and uninteresting? Showing fresh displays means that you're also updated with the latest events and seasons, like back-to-school themes and holiday breaks.

Use your mannequins properly to help your customers imagine what the clothes will look like. Plenty of times, clothing items beautifully displayed on mannequins increase how attractive it can be for a potential buyer. This also saves them the effort of imagining what the clothes would look like when worn.

Tell a story through visualization.

Have you ever walked through an IKEA store? Perhaps no other shop tells a story as well as this chain does. The minute you walk into a branch, you experience what it's like to actually imagine yourself living in the spaces, from bedrooms to living rooms, from kitchens to garages, from playrooms to offices. Each space tells a definite story, and it's all because of how well the items are positioned to engage all the senses and boost the shopping experience for every customer.

This effectively implants an important narrative into the customer's mind: what would it feel like if I had these things and lived in these spaces?

With static displays for your used clothes, remember to keep things straightforward and simple. You don't need to overwhelm your customers with all kinds of distractions—just highlight your key items and make the experience more streamlined. Focus on the message you want to portray, and keep it consistent. For instance, does this section of clothes provide an image of casual Sundays and brunch dates with friends? Or does one section showcase the different clothing items a customer can try on if they're getting ready to attend a formal evening event?

Think outside the box.

Just because you already have a signage outside that displays your logo and brand name doesn't mean you should stick to that alone! You can create some window displays to capture the attention of people who are passing by outside. Make sure that the displays are eye-catching, and that they also engage the senses. Use color theory.

Once the customer steps inside your store, make sure that you have enough engaging elements to keep them there! In-store signage is also important to keep your brand top-of-mind. If you have any ongoing promotions, make sure they're displayed loud and clear inside your shop. Just keep everything consistent and simple—it's never a good idea to overdo it and create more confusion for customers inside.

Here's an interesting display tactic you can use, if you have the space: create shelf guides or labels. If you want to categorize items based on when to wear them, you can use events to label your shelves with, like "Date Night", "Sunday Brunch", or "Fierce Workwear". You can even use labels as how-to guides! Imagine having one section that says, "Five Ways to Style Palazzo Pants" or "How to Rock Your Kimono Jacket from Morning 'til Night". You can even have a mini-area where your staff can demo certain items, like "Six Ways to Wear a Tie". It's all up to your imagination—and also about what gives value to your customers.

Of course, you have to make sure that everything that's written inside your store is clear and readable at first glance. The right font choice (and font size) is crucial, so you should steer clear of fancy script typefaces in general or poorly handwritten ones.

Physical and Online Sales Hybrid

Now, we've talked about the pros and cons of online shops and brick-and-mortar stores, but the thing is that you will be a more effective seller if you do both. E-commerce sales are growing every day, and because of how easy and cost-effective online stores can be, it's impossible not to think about having one. You can do both a physical shop and an online one if you have the resources—it's just good common sense!

You can use online channels to complement your brick-and-mortar daily operations, or vice versa. Here are just a few ways that can happen:

•   Customers may want to order online and pick up the items in person. They may want to check the condition of the clothes, or may want to fit them properly first. This can save both of your shipping costs.

•   A customer may want to reserve an item online but try it on first before finally deciding to buy them.

•   A customer may want to make use of online-only promotions or store-only promotions, either way.

It's important to remember that it's not a competition. You shouldn't be competing with your own online or physical store. You may also want to do a pop up store if you can't have a permanent physical shop. Pop up shops are good ways to have a physical presence without the exorbitant rental costs.

With a pop up store, you can give customers an avenue to see the clothes in person, and convert those buyers who just haven't gotten used to online shopping just yet. Pop ups are useful especially if you have seasonal items, which is exactly how selling apparel works. You can take advantage of holiday events, seasons, and peak times. You can join mall events, bazaars, community fairs, and so much more.

Pop ups can also help you reach new markets that you haven't reached with your online store before. Because these normally have other sellers in the area as well, don't think of them as your competition—think of them as a way to bring new target customers to your own brand. It's a great way to test out target markets as well if you're just starting out.

Here, you can physically see how customers react to your products, which ones attract them the most, and which items are the popular bestsellers. You can collate all of this information and mull over them when the event or pop up shop is over, and use that knowledge to improve your online store.

A pop up can also help you test out a certain location. You can try out the local community's response before you decide to make a bigger investment and rent or buy a permanent physical store in that area. And if nothing else, it's a great way to really get your hands dirty and get out there! With an online shop, there really aren't enough opportunities to interact with your loyal customers physically. With a pop up shop, you can do just that—you can meet loyal fans, garner new ones, and see for yourself just how the whole things plays out in actuality. The same is true with street fairs and bazaars.

Conclusion

There are so many ways you can succeed with your second-hand clothing shop, but the best thing you can do (and the most valuable experience you can get) is to go out and actually do it! Experience is always the best teacher. Until you get out and start selling, you will never be able to grasp fully everything that running a used clothing shop entails. Of course, the most important thing you can do is to be prepared for it, just so you know you're setting yourself up for success.

Pitfalls to avoid include not having a definitive source for your merchandise. In case you run out of things to sell, or your supplier doesn't deliver, how do you cope? How can you keep a good business continuity if you can't rake in any sales to help fund your operating costs?

Speaking of your business plan, we already talked about how to draft a good one, but let me say it again—create a good business plan. This just doesn't get said enough, and I have to repeat it to stress its importance. You need to plan, plan, plan. You need to plan your target market, plan your shop size (going for a huge shop size right off the bat is an amateur mistake!), plan your budget, plan your location, plan your website, plan your staffing and equipment, and plan your marketing and advertising strategies.

You can't have too many products, and you can't have too few, either. At first, you need to stick to the bestselling ones (actual apparel, hats, and accessories) before taking bigger and bigger risks as you go on. You can always have a niche market too—finding one is the challenge. This will really depend on what you have on-hand. If you were left with clothes from someone else, how can you categorize them into a cohesive theme? Can they be considered vintage, or are they just random pieces of clothing that are too far gone to resell? Are they still in good quality—good enough for a new owner to love it for years to come? Remember—just because you sell second-hand doesn't mean the clothes have to be second-rate!

Don't rush your brand—building a good reputation ad image takes time. Building customer loyalty takes a while too, so be patient! It's important to get valuable feedback (relevant feedback, may I add, and not just a "yes man" or a close family member or friend who won't have the heart to bring you down) when you're deciding on a brand name and a logo design.

It's also important to get the proper business licenses just so you won't encounter any legal issues further down the road. Have a personal Mr. or Mrs. Fix-It in all aspects, whether you need to have anything handy done or you need to get your papers in order. Remember—as your business grows bigger, you will likely be more and more preoccupied with a whole bunch of stuff, so little things tend to slip through the cracks. A good all-around manager or assistant can help you keep everything organized and help you be on top of everything.

You can't do it alone, but you can't hire the wrong people, either! Make sure that the staff you surround yourself with are competent—don't just pick the closest one who happens to be available at the time. This will prove to be more costly further down the line.

Remember to keep up with the trends as well! Just because you're running a second-hand clothing store doesn't mean everything has to be old and old-fashioned. Used clothing can be from any era, so it's important to stay up-to-date with everything that's going on in the fashion industry too.

That said, don't just focus on the products themselves. You should still be able to see the big picture, especially the bird's eye view of how your capital works and how budgets align.

It's also handy to know how your customers think and behave as they shop for used clothing. For online sites, they always want to factor in the shipping costs to their purchasing decisions. For instance, they will have to weigh whether or not it's worth it to buy a certain clothing item with the shipping cost on top of the selling price.

- Is it fair?

- Is it reasonable?

- Can I buy this same piece of clothing somewhere else?

- Is it more convenient to buy this here, or elsewhere?

- Will the delivery time be quick?

- Will it arrive on time, and are there rush fees/options in case I want to have the items on-hand in time for an event?

Before you launch your store (online or physical), build anticipation for it. Write blogs, invite people to a soft opening, or advertise on relevant sites or bazaars and street markets or fairs if you have the money. You can also rely on word-of-mouth if you've got a good social network or lots of family and friends. Then, when you feel like you've exhausted everything and you've made sure you're good to go, DO IT! Running your own second-hand clothing shop is tiring but rewarding, challenging but exciting, and stressful but fun. It's all of these conflicting emotions that you deal with every day, but it's also one of the most fulfilling passions you can ever monetize.

So, here's to you and your dream (and to Gran's clothes, where this all began). I hope that you're as excited as I am when I first started this venture. And when you're finally a big business mogul, I'd definitely love to hear from you. One way you can let me know if this book has helped you at all is to leave me a review wherever you purchased this book. Online reviews really help me reach a wider audience and enable me to keep writing future books.

I sincerely wish you the best of luck. Happy selling!